EMOTIONAL MATURITY

DR. SAVITA MISHRA

Contents

Preface *v*

1. Introduction 1

2. Reviews Of Related Literature 18

3. The Methodology 25

4. Collection And Organization Of Data 31

5. Analysis And Interpretation Of Data 52

6. Summary And Recommendation 63

Bibliography 71

Preface

The 21st century is an era of technological revolution. Due to the changes in the technology, the environment of today is changing as never before. College students of today are well and easily exposed to vast, unlimited and most importantly censored information and are subject to high pressure because of ever increasing competition and expectations from their family and peers. In this dynamic environment, many of the pupils are finding it difficult to adjust them and even sometimes succumb to the environmental pressure. This is quite evident from the increase in the number of criminal, suicidal, drug abuse and rape cases where adolescents are involved. In some extreme cases, college students are even being used by terrorist groups as a weapon of terror. All of it can be attributed to their low social and emotional maturity. At the end of the adolescent period, the teenagers are expected to be socially and emotionally mature, that is, they must be ready to face the world alone without their parents or teachers to act as buffers, as they did when they were a child. Since emotional and social maturity plays a vital role in transformation of young adolescents into an ideal citizen, therefore, the study of these parameters among adolescents is of great importance.

Dr. Savita Mishra

CHAPTER ONE

INTRODUCTION

Transition from school to college is a complex process for almost all students. Pascarella and Terenzini (1991) describe this transition as a "culture shock involving significant social and psychological relearning in the face of encounters with new ideas, new teachers and friends with quite varied values and beliefs, new freedoms and opportunities, and new academic, personal and social demands". Adjusting to college life immediately after school becomes a difficult transition for many students. The decision to go to college depends on many reasons. It can be for higher education, earning a degree, increasing knowledge or personal growth. Going to college gives a chance to the students to learn new things, meet new people, to deal effectively with new experiences and challenges which eventually help them in their personal growth and development. Tinto (1993) has proposed three stages that students move through from school to college i.e. separation, transition and incorporation. According to Astin's (1999) theory of involvement, a highly involved student is one who, for example, devotes considerable energy to studying, spends much time on campus, participates actively in student organizations, and interacts frequently with faculty members and other students. Adjustment difficulties arise from the differences between the expectations of the students and realities of college life. The nature of students expectations about university, and their relation with adjustment in university, were examined in a longitudinal investigation by (Jackson, Pancer, Pratt, & Hunsberger, 2000) . Students whose expectations were fearful reported more stress, depression, and poorer university adjustment than students with other types of expectations, particularly prepared. Also Mohan (1992) asserts that adjustment improves with age.

Adjustment to college and their increasing emotional maturity involves a variety of demands differing in kind and degree and requiring lot of coping responses or adjustments. It's not only academics with which the students are concerned; they are equally affected by the social and emotional changes. The first year students have an increased personal freedom where they have to make their own decisions and take the responsibility to maintain balance between various newfound demands. In college they are required to adjust to the new environment and to work out their concerns directly with the teachers. As far as the academic adjustment is concerned, students are expected to be independent learners in college where they need to adjust with the new academic demands. It is different from what they experienced in school because here they have to face more competition, deal with more academic load and to maintain pace with other students in the class they need to follow the different teaching styles. However, Sood (1992) found no significant relationship between achievement and adjustment. Students academic achievement throughout a period of one semester found to be significantly predicted by college overall adjustment, academic adjustment, and personal-emotional adjustment (Abdullah, Elias, Mahyuddin & Uli 2009).

For new students it is again important to adjust themselves with the social climate of the college. A major task for them is to learn to manage their feelings and to express them appropriately. Results of the study by Dyson and Renk (2006) on the relationship among the gender role, level of depressive symptomatology, and level of stress exhibited by college freshmen showed that all these factors are considered as important in facilitating their transition to university life. Masculinity significantly predicted problem-focused coping, and femininity significantly predicted emotion-focused coping. Tiwari and Pooranchand (1994) founded a significant difference between high and low achieving students in familial, social and emotional areas of adjustment. Enochs and Roland (2006) examined the relationship between living environment, gender, overall adjustment to college and social adjustment in freshmen's academic and overall adjustments. The study found that boys had significantly higher overall adjustment levels than girls regardless of living environment.

There is a paucity of research on assessing the adjustment processes and emotional aspects of students in colleges in India. Not much work done on student emotion, adjustment and related interventions. Deducing from above studies it has found that entering to college is considered as a time full of stress and strain many emotional and psychological issues are raised as a result. Since pursuing college degree students put their major time, energy and money into it, it is crucial to give proper attention to the problems related to adjustment among freshmen students. A major adjustment and emotional difficulty could mean an inability to graduate which in turn can affect their future.

The 21st century is an era of technological revolution. Due to the changes in the technology, the environment of today is changing as never before. College students of today are well and easily exposed to vast, unlimited and most importantly censored information and are subject to high pressure because of ever increasing competition and expectations from their family and peers. In this dynamic environment, many of the pupils are finding it difficult to adjust them and even sometimes succumb to the environmental pressure. This is quite evident from the increase in the number of criminal, suicidal, drug abuse and rape cases where adolescents are involved. In some extreme cases, college students are even being used by terrorist groups as a weapon of terror. All of it can be attributed to their low social and emotional maturity. At the end of the adolescent period, the teenagers are expected to be socially and emotionally mature, that is, they must be ready to face the world alone without their parents or teachers to act as buffers, as they did when they were a child. Since emotional and social maturity plays a vital role in transformation of young adolescents into an ideal citizen, therefore, the study of these parameters among adolescents is of great importance. Moreover, it is a general belief that gender difference exists in almost all developmental aspects of human being such as physical, social, emotional, cognitive etc.

"Emotions shape the landscape of our mental and social lives. Like the „geographical upheavals" a traveler might discover in a landscape where recently only a flat plane could be seen, they mark our lives as uneven, uncertain, and prone to reversal". (Nussbaum 2001) Life is becoming very fast with the advancement of science and technology. The 21st century is an era of technological revolution. Due to the technology, the environment is changing as never before. Youth as well as adults of today are well and easily exposed to vast, unlimited and most importantly censored information and are subject to high pressure because of ever increasing competition and expectations from their family and peers. Under this dynamic environment the youth as well as adults are finding it difficult to adjust them and even sometimes succumb to the environmental pressure. Though man has conquered time and space to a great extent by the present level of scientific advancement, yet there is great threat to his existence. The Indian society is becoming increasingly materialistic. The present generation is moving ahead to achieve their material gains by every means. They find it hard to bridge the gap between their head and heart. This puts them always in conflicting situations. For the personal happiness it is very important that you must be aware about yourself and must be able to tolerate a delay in the satisfaction of your needs. For this purpose you have to choose maturity, to behave in a consciously designed manner. Maturity is the ability to respond to the environment in an appropriate manner. This response is generally learned rather than instinctive. Maturity also encompasses being aware of the correct time and place to behave and knowing when to act, according to the circumstances and the culture of the society one lives in (David Wechsler 1950). According to Finley (1996), "Maturity is the capacity of mind to endure an ability of an individual to respond to uncertainty, circumstances or environment in an appropriate manner". As we discussed above that youths and adults are facing a lot of difficulties and pressures from the competitive materialistic world, so they are vulnerable to different psychological problems. Therefore, here the study of maturity in emotional aspect of personality is challenging our attention. Menninger (1999), Emotional maturity includes the ability to deal constructively with reality. Dosanjh (1960) "Emotional maturity means balanced personality. It means ability to govern disturbing emotion, show steadiness and endurance under pressure and be tolerant and free from neurotic tendency". Prof Y. Singh (1990) "Emotional maturity is not only the effective determinant of personality pattern but also helps to control the growth of an adolescent's development. A person who is able to keep his emotions under control, to brook delay and to suffer without self-pity might still be emotionally stunned". So emotionally mature person will have more satisfaction in life; he will be satisfied with what he is and have a balance between his head and heart.

1.1 CONCEPT OF EMOTION

Etymologically the word 'Emotion' is derived from the Latin word 'Emovere' which means to stir up, to excite or to agitate. According to Charles E Skinner, An emotionally matured person is the one who is able to keep a lid on his feelings. He can suffer in silence; he can bide his time in spite of present discomfort. He is not subject to swings in mood, he is not volatile. When he does express emotion, he does so with moderation, decency and in good order.

A. Emotion is the energy which makes the mind work — it supplies the energy for survival.

1. Emotions — physical and mental feelings — are necessary for life and stimulate you to behave in a certain way
2. In that sense, we are all emotional people.

B. There is a difference, however, between emotional maturity and immaturity.

1. The difference lies in whether you let this energy (emotion) rule you to your own hurt and the hurt of others, or whether you, through careful thought, put it to use constructively
2. You can't stop the energy that is emotion, but you can control and direct it into constructive channels.

C. How to control emotion.

1. Realize there are negative and positive ways to react to an impulse that comes into your mind.
2. Understand that you have been programmed from infancy to react the way you presently do.
3. Realize, further, you can develop the ability to choose the way you want to react, rather than allowing it to be automatic. In other words, you can reprogram your behavior.
4. The following quote shows how this process works. "Once the lever has been pulled, the water (emotion) rushes on inevitably. There are, however, several channels in which the stream may be diverted, labeled: brave, fairly brave, cowardly, stupid, smart, immature; and the individual has the power to direct the stream, so that even though he cannot stem the tide, he can cause it to flow in the channel of his choice."(Discovering Ourselves, Edward A. Strecker and Kenneth Appel).

1. CATEGORIES OF EMOTIONS:

Harold Schlosberg speaks of three basic dimensions of emotions. a) Pleasantness – unpleasantness b) Attention – Rejection c) Level of activation (Sleep - Tension) Others add a fourth dimension to the above three – degree of complexity. When these 4 bipolar dimensions are imposed upon the possible emotional states, we get several categories of emotions.

a) Primary goal oriented emotions (anger, joy, fear and grief are also called PRIMARY or basic emotions) b) Emotions triggered by sensory stimulation (pain, disgust and delight) c) Emotions related to others (love, envy and pity) d) Appreciative emotions (wonder and awe) e) Emotions pertaining to self- appraisal and related to one's level of aspiration (Pride, shame and guilt) All these increasingly varied and differentiated patterns of emotional expressions are gradually evolved in the course of development and learning from the initial single generalized emotional response of excitement of the new born infant.

1. **THE NATURE OF EMOTIONS:**

Feelings and emotions are strictly subjective, individual, personal, intimate experiences. Feelings are always present in conscious liking and denote states of satisfaction or dissatisfaction, liking or disliking anything. Emotions are more complex than feelings and involve feelings, impulses to action and adjustment, and bodily changes and excitement. In order to understand the educational significance of emotions and their development, it is essential to lay down criteria for distinguishing between emotional and non-emotional experiences.

a. Emotion is stirred-up condition involving disturbance, excitement, conflict or tension in behavior. In an emotional situation, some stimulus arouses or stirs emotions into action.
b. An emotion is brought into action by the perception of some stimulus. Psychologically it is a complex experience involving perception and widespread characteristic bodily changes in the action of muscles, glands and the automatic nervous system.
c. Every emotional state involves an impulse to action. There is a drive toward some kind of adjustment, to obtain satisfaction, to effect destruction or escape or to gratify a desire. The emotion subsides to the extent to which adjustments are achieved.

1.1.3 EFFECTS OF EMOTIONS:

a. Emotions provide energy to an individual to face a particular situation.
b. Emotions work as motivators of our behavior.
c. Emotions influence our adjustment in the society.
d. High emotional conditions disturb the mental equilibrium of an individual.
e. High emotional conditions disturb the reasoning and thinking of an individual.

1.2 MATURITY

The concept of maturity has not received a great deal of explicit attention in the literature. Delineation of libidinal development has been yielded the important formulation of the "Genital level" and "objective-interest (Freud, 1924). Recent emphasis on the conflict between the regressive, dependents, versus the progressive, productive forces in the personality has directed interest toward the more detailed nature of maturity.

1.2.1 NATURE OF MATURITY

1. One of the most obvious pathways of development, long emphasized by Sigmund Freud and Franz Alexander, is from the parasitic dependence of the fetus to the relative independence of parent, with parental capacity for responsibility for spouse and child.
2. Intimately bound-up with the organism's development from parasitism on the mother to relative independence from the parents is its increased capacity for responsibility and productivity and its decreased receptive needs. Children learn to control their hostilities, their sexuality and other impulses, and to develop the orientations of maturity largely through the incentive of being loved.
3. Maturity is relative freedom from the well-know constellation of inferiority, egotism, and competitiveness.
4. Another aspect of maturity consists in the conditioning and the training necessary for socialization and domestication.
5. Hostile aggressiveness, using the term to include all sorts of anger, hate, cruelty and belligerency, is always a sign of emotional irritation and threat.
6. Another important attribute of maturity is a firm sense of reality.
7. Another characteristic of maturity is flexibility and adaptability.

1.3 EMOTIONAL MATURITY

In the present circumstances, youth as well as children are facing difficulties in life. These difficulties are giving rise to many psycho-somatic problems such as anxiety, tensions, frustrations and emotional upsets in day to day life. So, the study of emotional life is now emerging as a descriptive science, comparable with anatomy. It deals with interplay of forces with intensities and quantities. Available tests are crude and measure chiefly the degree of dependence. But this test measures the different aspects of emotional maturity. As self acceptance is an important aspect of maturity says Wenkart, and it must be preceded by acceptance from others.

Emotional maturity is defined as, "A process in which the personality is continually striving for greater sense of emotional health, both intra-psychically and intra-personally". In brief emotional maturity can be called as the process of impulse control through the agency of "self" or "ego". Actually, emotional maturity is not only the effective determinant of personality pattern but it also helps to control the growth of adolescent's development. The concept "Mature" emotional behavior of any level is that which reflects the fruits of normal emotional development. A person who is able to keep his emotions under control i.e., able to break delay and to suffer without self-pity, might still be emotionally stunned and childish. Morgan (1934) stated the view that an adequate theory of emotional maturity must take account of the full scope of the individuality, power and his ability to enjoy the use of his powers. According to Walter D Smithson (1974) emotional maturity is a process in which the personality is continuously striving for greater sense of emotional health, both intra-psychically and intra-personality. Kaplan and Baron elaborate the characteristics of an emotionally mature person; say that he has the capacity to withstand delay in satisfaction of needs. He has the ability to tolerate a reasonable amount of frustration. He has belief in long-term planning and is capable of delaying or revising his expectations in terms of demands of situations. An emotionally mature child has the capacity to make effective adjustment with himself, members of his family his peers in the school, society and culture. But maturity means not merely the capacity for such attitude and functioning but also the ability to enjoy them fully.

L.S Hollingsworth (1928) mentions some characteristics of emotionally mature person in the following points-

i. He is capable of responding in gradation or degree of emotional responses. He does not respond in all or none fashion, but keeps within bounds. If his hat blows off, he does not blow up.
ii. He is also able to delay his responses as controlled with the impulsiveness of young child.
iii. Handling of self pity, instead of showing unrestrained self pity, he tries to feel for him.

Childhood emotional stresses influence the infant's congenital heredity plus physical and emotional forces acting upon sperm and egg (prior to conception and until birth) endowment and development forces, the child being most formative up to the age of about six.

The most outstanding mark of emotional maturity, accordance to Cole (1944) is ability to bear tension. Other marks are an indifference toward certain kinds of stimuli that affect the child o adolescent and he develops moodiness and sentimentally. Besides, emotionally matured person persist the capacity for fun and recreation. He enjoys both play and responsibility activities and keep them in proper balance. According to Fred McKinney, "The characteristics of an emotionally mature are hetero-sexuality, appreciation of attitude and behavior of others, tendency to adopt the attitudes and habits of others and capacity to delay his own responses."

Therefore, the emotionally mature is not one who necessarily has resolved all conditions that aroused anxiety and hostility but it is continuously in process of seeing himself in clear perspective, continually involved in a struggle to gain healthy integration of feeling, thinking action.

1.3.1 SIGNS OF EMOTIONAL MATURITY

Each person has a different level of emotional maturity. It is something which you can consistently work on and improve over time. You can use the following signs of emotional maturity to gauge your own level:

a. **Flexibility:** You are able to see each situation as unique and you can adapt your style accordingly.
b. **Responsibility:** You take responsibility for your own life. You understand that your current circumstances are a result of the decisions you have taken up to now. When something goes wrong, you do not rush to blame others. You identify what you can do differently the next time and develop a plan to implement these changes.

c. **You understand that vision trumps knowledge:** You know that you do not need to have all the answers. As long as you can identify the problem, you can visualize a solution and research the best way to implement that solution.
d. **Personal growth:** Meeting the challenges of tomorrow requires learning and development today. You have a desire to learn and a thirst for knowledge. Learning and development activities form a key part of your schedule.
e. **You seek alternative views:** Knowing that the way things are done can always be improved, you willingly seek out the opinions and views of others. You do not feel threatened when people disagree with you. If you feel that their way is better, you are happy to run with it.
f. **Non-judgmental:** Variety makes the world a more beautiful place. Even when you disagree with people, you do not feel the need to criticize them. Instead, you respect their right to their beliefs.
g. **Resilience:** There will always be things that go wrong. There will always be setbacks and major disappointments. While you may initially be a little upset, emotional maturity allows you to express your feelings, identify the actions you can take, and move on.
h. **A calm demeanor:** It's hard to be calm 100% of the time but you are able to remain calm the majority of the time.
a. **Realistic optimism:** You are not deluded. You know that success requires effort and patience. You do, though, have an optimistic disposition whereby you believe you can cope with whatever life throws at you. You also believe that there are opportunities out there for you, so you seek them out.
j. **Approachability:** You are usually easy to get along with and people feel comfortable approaching you. Building relationships is never contrived; it comes easy to you.
k. **Self-belief:** You appreciate when others praise or compliment you. It feels good when they approve. However, you know that there will always be people who disapprove but you are confident in who you are and what you do. If you believe that a particular course of action is right for you, you will do it, whether they approve or not.
ax. **Humors:** You don't take yourself too seriously. You are able to enjoy a good laugh with friends and colleagues, even when you are the butt of the joke.

One of the greatest obstacles to emotional maturity is passive aggressive behavior. You can learn to overcome it without guide to Tackling Passive Aggressive Behaviors. Emotional maturity allows you to take charge of your life. You have your own vision for your life and your own ambition for success. Focusing on realizing your vision, you can create a happy, healthy life where you respect yourself and others. When you develop emotional maturity, life becomes a joy rather than a chore. Your happiness and fulfillment are in your hands. Emotional maturity doesn't evolve overnight. It takes effort, practice and patience. If you can improve a little every day, you will soon be living a happier, more fulfilled life.

1.3.2 LEVELS OF EMOTIONAL MATURITY

Generally there are six levels of Emotional Maturity. They are as follows:

i. **Basic Emotional Responsibility**- When a person reaches level one of emotional maturity, they realize that they can no longer view their emotional states as the responsibility of external forces such as people, places, things, forces, fate, and spirits. They learn to drop expressions from their speech that show disowner ship of feelings and a helpless or victim attitude towards their feelings.

ii. **Emotional Honesty**- Emotional honesty concerns the willingness of the person to know their own feelings. This is a necessary step to self-understanding and acceptance. They are related solely to the person's conscious and unconscious fears of dealing directly with the critical voices they hear inside.

iii. **Emotional Openness**- This level concerns the person's willingness and skills in sharing their feelings in an appropriate manner and at appropriate times. Persons at this level experience and learn the value of ventilating feelings, and also the dangers involved in hiding feelings from self and others. At this level, one has the openness, the freedom to experience any emotion without the need, the compulsion to suppress or repress it.

iv. **Emotional Assertiveness**- The person at this level of work enters a new era of positive self-expression. The primary goal here is to be able to ask for and to receive the nurturing that one needs and wants— first from self and then from others. As a secondary goal, persons should learn how to express any feeling appropriately in any situation, i.e., without aggressive overtones. This person makes time for their feelings— they prize and respect them. Such understand the connection between suppressed feelings, stress, and illness.

v. **Emotional Understanding**- Persons on this level understand the actual cause and effect process of emotional responsibility and irresponsibility. Self-concepts are known as "the" problem. They realize that it is not possible to have a so- called good self-concept without a complimentary bad self- concept. Such experience firsthand, that because of the nature of knowledge and the formation of self-concepts, that all self- concepts contain their opposites.

vi. **Emotional Detachment**- At this level the person lives without the burden and snare of self-concepts, self-images, self-constructs, and all group-concepts and thing-concepts. They are only aware of self as process, as a sensing being, as an experiencing being, as a living vessel, as unknowable and untrappable because it is alive and not static or fixed. True detachment from all self-concepts has occurred. Thus true detachment from others has also occurred, which means that absolute emotional responsibility has been achieved.

1.3.3 DEVELOPMENT OF EMOTIONAL MATURITY

Emotional Development is one of the major aspects of human growth and development. Emotions like anger, fear, love etc. play a great role in the development of child's personality. Not only his physical growth and development is linked with his emotional makeup, but his intellectual, social, moral and aesthetic development are also controlled by his emotional behavior and experiences. The overall importance of emotional experiences in the life of a human being makes it quite essential to know about the emotions.

1. Emotional development during infancy: Form his very birth, the infant cries and his bodily movements seem to give evidence of the presence of emotional element in him.

2. Emotional development during childhood: In the infancy, the child is only concerned with his own well being. Therefore, the emotions are generally aroused by the conditions which are related with his immediate well-being. But as he grows, his world grows large and he has to respond to a variety of stimuli.

During childhood, peer group relationship and school atmosphere and other environmental factors influence his emotional behaviour. His emotions get linked with the new experiences and interest and his emotional behaviour gets linked with the new stimuli. At the same time he does not react to old stimuli. For example, he does not show anger at being dressed or bathed, neither does he show any fear of stranger.

3. Emotional development during adolescence: The emotional balance is once again disturbed in adolescence. The individual once again experiences the violent and intensive current of emotional experiences with regard to emotional experiences. This is the period of intensive storm and stress. At no stage this emotional energy is as strong and dangerous as in adolescence. It is very difficult for a adolescent to exercise control over his emotions. The sudden functioning of sexual glands and tremendous increase in physical energy makes him restless. Moreover, adolescents are not consistent in their emotions. Emotions during this stage fluctuate very frequently and quickly. It makes them moody. Sometimes they are very happy and at another time they are extremely sad and all this happens in a very short time. So there is too much uncertainty in the nature of their emotional states.

4. Emotional development in adulthood: Emotional development reaches its maximum in adulthood. During this stage, generally all individuals attain emotional maturity.

1.3.4 FACTORS AFFECTING EMOTIONAL MATURITY

a) Health and physical Development of an Individual: There is a positive correlation between health and physical and emotional development. Children who are physically weak or who suffer from occasional illness are more emotionally upset. Any abnormal increase or decrease in the functioning of glands creates obstacles in the proper emotional development.

b) Family environment and emotional development: A cordial healthy relationship between the parents is very conducive for the emotional development of the child. The order of birth, size of the family, discipline in the family, the parental attitude towards the child (pampered, overprotected or neglected) are all important factors in the emotional development of the child.

c) School Environment: The attitude of the teachers, school discipline, academic facilities available, physical facilities, methods of teaching, co-curricular activities, etc, all play a pivotal role in developing emotional maturity.

d) Peer group relationship and emotional development: The influence of the classmates and other members of the group affect emotional maturity.

e) Intelligence and Emotional Development: H. Meltzer (1937) as quoted by E.B. Hurlock has observed, "There is less emotional control on an average, among the children of lower intellectual level, than among children of the same group who are bright. An intelligent person, with his thinking and reasoning powers, is in a better position to exercise control over his emotions."

f) Neighborhood, community and society's environmental influence and emotional development: The child lives in the society and inherits so many traits of his emotional behavior from the surrounding.

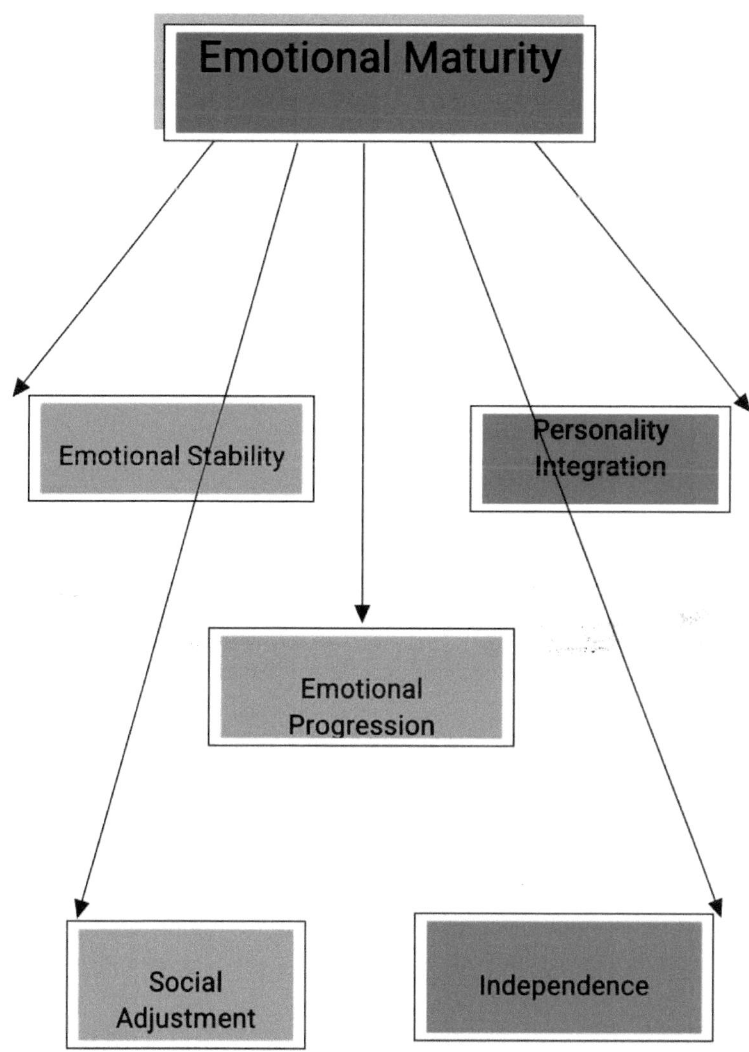

Figure (i) Details of the Component that have been studied

1.3.5 COMPONENTS OF EMOTIONAL MATURITY

a. **Emotional Stability**

Emotional stability refers to the characteristics of a person that does not allow him to react excessively or given to swings in mood or marked changes in any emotive situation. The emotionally stable person is able to do what is required of him in any given situation. Contrary to it, emotional instability is a tendency to quick changing and unreliable responses and is a factor representing syndrome of irritability, stubbornness, temper tantrums, lack of capacity to dispose of problems an seeks help for one's day to day problem. In another word "emotional stability" refers to a person's ability to remain calm or even keel when faced with pressure or stress. Basically a lack of emotional stability means someone feels more emotional highs and emotional lows.

b. **Emotional Progression**

Emotional Progression is the characteristics of a person that refers to a feeling of adequate advancement and growing vitality of emotions in relation to the environment to ensure a positive thinking imbued with righteousness and contentment. Whereas emotional regression is also a broad group of factors representing such syndromes as feeling of inferiority, restlessness, hostility, aggressiveness, and self-centeredness. This factor has correlation with total score on the scale. On inter-correlation matrix, it is highly inter-correlated with other two factors, that of personality disintegration and lack of independence, but has low inter correlations with those of emotional instability and social maladjustment factors. This has emerged as the broadest factor in the scale. It has high inter correlations with personality disintegration, lack of independence and low inter correlation with social maladjustment and emotional instability. It also has a high correlation with the total score on all the five factors of the scale.

c. **Social Adjustment**

Social Adjustment refers to a process of interaction between the needs of a person and demands of the social environment in any given situation, so that they can maintain and adapt a desired relationship with environment. Therefore, it may be described as a person's harmonious relationship with his social world. Whereas socially maladjusted person shows lack of social adaptability should hatred, reclusive but boasting, liar and shirker.

d. **Personality Integration**

Personality integration is the process of unifying the diverse elements of an individual's motives and dynamic tendencies, resulting in harmonious co-actions and de-escalation of the inner conflict (English and English, 1958) in the undaunted expression of behavior, whereas disintegrated personality includes all those symptoms, like reaction, phobias formation, realization, pessimism, immortality etc. such a person suffers from inferiorities and hence reacts to environment through aggressiveness, destruction and has distorted sense of reality. In brief, such a person shows varied degrees of neuroticism.

e. **Independence**

Independence is the capacity of a person's attitudinal tendency to be self reliant or of resistance to control by others, where he can take his decisions by his own judgment based on facts by utilizing his intellectual and creative potentialities. He would never like to show any habitual reliance upon another person in making his decisions or carrying out difficult actions, whereas a depended person shows parasitic dependence on other is egotic and lacks 'objective interests'. People think of him an unreliable person.

CHAPTER TWO

REVIEWS OF RELATED LITERATURE

Under this section, a detailed review of earlier researches has been presented in accordance with the prescriptions made in APA manual 1994. The materials have been presented year-wise, variable wise and national researchers an international researcher finding in seriatim:

2.1 STUDIES CONDUCTED IN INDIA

Kaur (1982) made a study on relationship between emotional maturity and teaching attitude of teacher-trainees. She concluded that there is positive co-relation between two variables.

Kaur (1984) conducted a study to see the effect of intelligence and emotional maturity on academic achievement of graduate level students and concluded that there was somewhat significant differences exist among science and arts students with respect to intelligence and emotional maturity.

Arya (1984) conducted a study on emotional maturity and values of superior children in family. He found that boys and girls of superior intelligence have better emotional maturity. Superior intelligence boys did well on the emotional maturity than girls of superior intelligence. Residence (urban, semi-urban and rural) did not have any link with emotional maturity.

Kaur (1995) conducted a study on the impact of attitudes of violence and non-violence on the levels of emotional maturity and adjustment patterns of college going students. She found that most of the colleges going girls were more emotionally stable as compared to college going boy.

Adhikari (1998) studied the difference in emotional maturity between University students and University teachers in India. The emotional maturity scores of male teachers and females teachers were higher than those of the 55 students.

Anju (2000) found that there exists a positive and significant relationship between emotional maturity and intelligence of student which implies that more intelligent the person is, more emotional mature he is. The relationship between emotional maturity and intelligence of girls came out to be significant.

Jha (2002) conducted a research on impact of emotional maturity on style of decision making and found that emotional maturity was positively associated with vigilant style of decision making in the case of college students.

Aleen and Sheema (2005) conducted a study on emotional stability among male and female students and had found that there was a significant difference between the mean scores of male and female students on emotional stability. Female students were less emotionally stable compared to male students.

Vijaylaxmi (2006) conducted a study on impact of emotional maturity on stress and self confidence of adolescents and found that adolescents with high emotional maturity had significantly higher stress and self confidence than those with lower emotional maturity.

Sivakumar (2010) conducted a study on influence of sex, community and family type on emotional maturity and found that the sex, community and the family type they belong did not play any role (no significant difference) in the emotional maturity of the college students. But it was inferred from that the religion the college students belongs to shows significant difference in their emotional maturity.

Jadhav (2010) conducted a research on the relationship between home environment and emotional maturity among college going students of Belgaum District in Karnataka and it was found that, there was no positive and significant relationship between home environment and emotional maturity among the urban students, studying in government colleges, with high socio-economic status and students less than 20 years of age.

Subbarayan, Visvanathan (2011) intended to measure the emotional maturity of college students. The result of the study showed that the emotional maturity of college students was extremely unstable. It was also found that the sex, community and the family type did not play any role in the emotional maturity of the college students.

Mahmoudi (2012) conducted a study to see the Emotional maturity and adjustment level of college students and stated that high positive correlation was obtained between emotional maturity and overall adjustment.

Sharma (2012) studied that there was an influence of adjustment and emotional maturity among first year college students. Results indicated that the first year undergraduate students were less emotionally mature, and had difficulty in adjusting emotionally and socially to the changing demands of the environment and faced more academic difficulty as compared to final year students. The final year students were more socially adjusted and more integrated into the social fabric of the college.

Aashra, Jogsan (2013) studied influence of emotional maturity and self-actualization in graduate and post-graduate students and found that there was significant difference in emotional maturity among graduate and post-graduate students. There was significant difference in self-actualization among graduate and post-graduate students.

Punithavathi (2013) studied the emotional maturity and decision making styles among arts and science and engineering college women students. The results revealed that there was significant difference between day scholars and hostellers women students in their emotional maturity and decision making styles with respect to their dwellings. The mean difference of the day scholars were higher than that of hostellers. Day scholars were vigilant and adaptable to their environment.

Nuzhat (2013) conducted a comparative study on emotional maturity of male and female Kashmir university of India distance learners. The results reveal that the Female University distance learners and Male University distance learners did not differ significantly on emotional maturity so far as composite score is concerned. However, on factor wise of emotional maturity scale Female University distance learners had **emotional instability** (factor 01) than Male University distance learners. They had lack of capacity to dispose of problems, irritability and needs constant help for one's day to day work, venerability, stubbornness and temper tantrum. Male University distance learners had **emotional regression** (factor 02) than female university distance learners. Male University Distance Learners had inferiority complex, restlessness, hostility, aggressiveness and self centeredness of being pursuing education through distance mode. They experience a sense of discomfort and lack of peace of mind. And on other factors their emotional maturity was almost same.

Sinha (2014) studied the relationship between emotional maturity and adjustment of college students to see the impact of gender on emotional maturity and adjustment. The result revealed that 1) Level of emotional maturity and adjustment of students were positively correlated. 2) There were significant differences between boys and girls student in term of their emotional maturity and adjustment viewpoint.

Kumar (2014) discloses that a significant correlation exists between emotional maturity and family relationship. From the review of different sources it was found that no comprehensive study was conducted on the university students and the investigator makes an effort to identify the level of emotional maturity in university students, keeping in view their level of education.

Wani, Masih (2015) studied emotional maturity across gender and level of education and found that male students are emotionally immature than females on personality disintegration dimension of emotional maturity. Significant difference was also found between post graduates and research scholars on personality disintegration dimension of emotional maturity. On other dimensions of emotional maturity no difference was found between males and females and post graduates and research scholars University students must be taught to identify their level of emotional maturity, as they are at the highest seat of learning. She also summarized that 'emotional maturity is the ability to govern disturbing emotions.

2.2 STUDY CONDUCTED ABROAD

Deand, & Bruton (1989) concluded that Emotional maturity was related to better marital adjustment.

Stephen(2002) conducted a study related to neuroticism and emotional maturity among college female students and found that the individuals who scored higher neuroticism were having a low level of emotional maturity.

Landry and Darroch (2002) in his research topic 'Journal Summary on Emotional Education' said that, environmental factors do affect the physical and emotional maturity of child.

Lichtenberg (2005) conducted a study on 'Emotional Maturity across Life Span' and found that only that man had ability to work with others who had emotional maturity and stability. He focused on ageing as well as personality and emotional maturity across 57 life span in his research work.

Nelson (2005) in his research related to 'Emotional Intelligence and Emotional Maturity' says that if we want our children to be emotionally mature, we must focus on their early childhood education; which affect certain level of social and emotional maturity.

Louis and Doss (2007) concluded that emotional maturity of P.G. students is influenced by sex, class and group. The level of emotional maturity of female students was higher than that of the male students.

2.3 RATIONALE OF THE STUDY

The specific needs for identifying these phenomena of Emotional Maturity as a natural and inevitable essential outcome of student growth and development rather than among pathological symptom. The Emotional maturity becomes important in the behavior of individuals. As the students are the pillars of the future generations their value pattern of Emotional Maturity are vital. So the present study intends to measure the Emotional Maturity of college students.

As has been described by **Edward E. Morler,** "Children and adolescents are driven by genes and hormones. However, beyond adolescence, an individual has to choose maturity. While emotional intelligence can be learned, emotional maturity is a choice. If it is not consciously made, the individual will not move beyond the emotional immaturity of an adolescent despite any and all trappings of material success". Emotional maturity is not something that necessarily grows with chronological age; we don't get more emotionally mature when we get older. Some adults are very emotionally immature and some have never matured. Hence they all find it difficult to adjust themselves with the changing environment of this scientific age. Therefore it is the dire need of the hour that our adolescents and adults should have proper emotional development to rightly channelize their emotions. Emotional maturity becomes very important in the behavior of the individuals, as students are the pillars of the nation and future generations, so their level of emotional maturity becomes very vital. This study is of significant value for students, families, teachers and administrators, as they can be made aware about the level of emotional maturity of their grown up youths. It will be quite helpful for post graduates and research scholars, who are at the highest seats of learning in universities to pay a good time of attention to their emotional maturity and make successful adjustments, whatever the situations are. Study will also try to make adolescents and adults to realize that becoming emotionally mature means becoming aware of their choices and their impacts. Being a post graduate or a researcher doesn't necessarily make a person capable of handling the situations. Therefore need was felt to study the level of emotional maturity of university students across gender and their level of education. While doing the research, the researcher will try to answer the following queries:

- Are the college students emotionally stable in relation to gender and age variation?
- Are the college students emotionally progressed in relation to gender and age variation?
- Are the college students socially adjusted in relation to gender and age variation?
- Do the college students have personality integration in relation to gender and age variation?
- Are the college students independent in relation to gender and age variation?

2.5 OBJECTIVES OF THE STUDY

The objectives of the study are:

- To study the emotional stability of college students in relation to gender and age variation.
- To study the emotional progression of college students in relation to gender and age variation.
- To study the social adjustment of college students in relation to gender and age variation.
- To study the personality integration of college students in relation to gender and age variation.
- To study the independence of college students in relation to gender and age variation.

2.6 HYPOTHESIS OF THE STUDY

The following null hypotheses are formulated for the research topic:

Ho_1 : There will be no significant difference in the emotional stability of college students in relation to gender variation.

Ho_2: There will be no significant difference in the emotional stability of college students in relation to age variation.

Ho_3: There will be no significant difference in the emotional progression of college students in relation to gender variation.

Ho_4: There will be no significant difference in the emotional progression of college students in relation to age variation.

Ho_5: There will be no significant difference in the social adjustment of college students in relation to gender variation.

Ho_6: There will be no significant difference in the social adjustment of college students in relation to age variation.

Ho_7: There will be no significant difference in the personality integration of college students in relation to gender variation.

Ho_8: There will be no significant difference in the personality integration of college students in relation to age variation.

Ho_9: There will be no significant difference in the independence of college students in relation to gender variation.

Ho_{10}: There will be no significant difference in the independence of college students in relation to age variation.

2.7 OPERATIONAL DEFINITION

Emotional Maturity: Emotional Maturity is a process in which the personality is continuously striving for greater sense of emotional health, both intra-psychically and intra-personally (Singh and Bharagava, 2005).

College Students: It refers to the students studying in different government and private colleges.

2.8 SCOPE AND DELIMITATION OF THE STUDY

The scope of the study is to analyze the emotional maturity of college students of West Bengal. The study will be delimited to 100 students selected from 4 colleges of West Bengal.

CHAPTER THREE

THE METHODOLOGY

This chapters have been made to highlight on the methodology adopted for conducting the study. So this section presents a brief outline of the design adopted, the sample selected, description of the tool used for study, technique of data analysis and procedure.

3.1 DESIGN

The purpose of the study was to find out the emotional maturity of college students. The design was descriptive method i.e., normative survey design. Here in the study, emotional maturity of college students has been studied in relation to gender and age. Therefore it was an ex-post-facto study for the fact that emotional maturity and other variables would be studied as they were. The other methods like historical, experimental study were not adopted on the following ground.

Application of historical method of research was not thought to be appropriate because the historical method of research was ideally suited for a study which was interested in analyzing a phenomenon, event or conditions in the context of forces and factors which operated in the past. For this it makes use of external and internal evidences as well as the primary and secondary sources of information. As it was confined for studying emotional maturity of college students under the present condition, a survey study seemed to be more appropriate.

The experimental method was also not considered suitable. The experimental method would have been adopted, if the predictors influence on the criterion would have been found out under controlled situations. In that case, the necessity of increasing or reducing the intensity of the independent variables would have been required. But the objectives of the present study did not show any increase or decrease in the strength of the independent variables as it was neither possible nor practicable to control the independent variables. Therefore the use of experimental method in this study was not seemed proper to be adopted.

The descriptive study collects three types of information. They are: what exists, what we want and how to reach the goals. The present study is related to gathering of evidences in the existing situation. In this present study, neither a historical trend is developed nor manipulation of independent variables. A co-relation design will be adopted. The study is descriptive study of ex-post-facto type. Only a normative survey has been conducted and analyzed in accordance with the variables of gender and age as an independent variable and emotional maturity as a dependent variable.

3.2 SAMPLE

The sample for the investigation comprised 100 male and female from different government and private colleges from West Bengal on simple random basis. The procedure adopted for the sampling design has been described here under. The simple random sampling procedure had been adopted for the investigation.

There are many techniques of sampling. This investigator adopted the techniques of simple random sampling and selected four colleges of different area. The total samples were 100 students. While selecting the sample, care was taken to have representative sample based on age above 21 and below 21 and gender i.e. male and female.

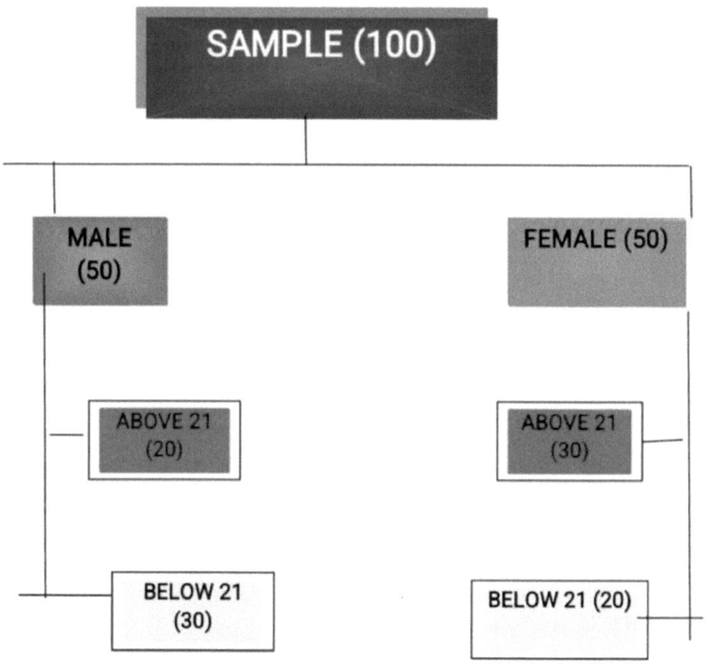

Figure: (ii) Details of the Sample

Table 1: Details of the sample

Sl. No.	Colleges	No. of Male	No. of Female	Total
1	Siliguri College	16	20	36
2	Kalipada Ghosh Tarai Mohabidyalaya, Bagdogra	14	13	27
3	St. Xevier's College	11	12	23
4	Silesian College	9	5	14
Total		50	50	100

After selecting a sample of 100 out of which 50 are male and 50 are female the investigator had categorized them under age variable i.e. above 21 and below 21 as per the requirement of the study.

3.3 TOOL USED

For the purpose of data collection questionnaire developed in National Psychology Corporation, Agra, by Singh and Bhargava (1984). It consists of five parts (component wise) and total 48 test items:

Table 2: Details of the Items (Component wise)

Sr. No	Areas or Components	Total No. of Items
a	Emotional Stability	10
b	Emotional Progression	10
c	Social Adjustment	10
d	Personality Integration	10
e	Independence	8
	TOTAL	**48**

Table No-3

Details of Scoring

V. Much	Much	Undecided	Probably	Never
5	4	3	2	1

The items are so stated that if the answer is very much a score of 5 is given ; for much 4 ; for undecided 3 ; and for probably 2 and for negative answer of never a score of 1 is awarded. Therefore, total score on the scale is indicative of emotional maturity whereas the greater the total score on the scale is expressed in terms of emotional immaturity.

3.4 TECHNIQUE OF DATA ANALYSIS

The data for the present study was collected through the use of the given tool. The data was scored manually and organized into frequency distribution tables, component wise, sub sample wise and totally. Questionnaire technique was adopted for data collection, scoring will be done according to the manual prescribed.

For the analysis purpose, both descriptive and inferential statistics were adopted. Descriptive statistics of measures of central tendency and measure of variability were calculated to assess the emotional maturity of college students. "t" ratio was calculated to find out intra difference in maturity due to gender and age variation.

The techniques of data analysis were followed as under:

- Mean and SD were calculated to describe the nature of the data
- "t" test was used to find the significant difference between the sub-samples an age and gender variation on five dimensions of emotional maturity in the scale $EMS\text{-}_{SB}$

3.5. PROCEDURES

Procedures adopted for obtaining data, its analysis and interpretations were delineated below:

- Administration of the questionnaire over a sample of 100 college students selected on simple random basis;

- Scoring as per manuals;
- Data collection-scores had been tabulated on a data sheet according to the variables under study
- Variable analysis had been made through "t" test;
- Results had been discussed in accordance with the Hypotheses;
- Results had been interpreted after scoring the test by descriptive and inferential statistics. Also by making corroboration of earlier studies with the present findings;
- A brief summary with conclusion and implications for further research had been given at the end;
- At last references and appendices had been added to the report.

CHAPTER FOUR

COLLECTION AND ORGANIZATION OF DATA

This chapter is devoted to presentation of the data in an organized form for verification of the hypotheses and interpretation of the result emerging out of the findings. Therefore, the present chapter was discussed under two heads, administration and scoring and organization of data. Under administration and scoring, the principles of administration of scales, scoring and preparation of data sheet are covered. Under organization of data, all the variables were subjected for descriptive measures through mean, median, mode and standard deviations. The details of the procedures were described as per the following.

4.1. ADMINISTRATION OF THE SCALE

ADMINISTRATION OF THE EMOTIONAL MATURITY SCALE (EMS-$_{SB}$)

The scale was administered over a sample of 100 college students. The following principles of administration of a test wise strictly followed.

i. The investigator first of all sought for the permission of the administration of the same from the heads of the institution;
ii. Rapport was established between the investigator and the students and it was made clear to the students that neither it was meant for examining them nor for utilizing the same for any other purpose rather than research. Orientation in this regard made the students tension free;
iii. The students who agreed to the proposal were selected for the administration of the questionnaire. There was no compulsion nor any restriction imposed on them;
iv. Preliminary consideration for administration of a questionnaire were made like free ventilation, good sitting accommodation and undisturbed

zone of the institution;

v. A placard containing 'Don't Disturb' was hung on the door of the examination hall;

vi. Students were given all information and clarification for responding of the items of the caste;

vii. The time-period for administration was chosen in such a way so that there was no possibility for any disturbance i.e. the time fixed for administration was neither before or after lunch nor before or after any amusement activity. It must usually do at the early sessions.

viii. All the students were provided with answer sheets and pencils;

ix. They were told to record their responses on the spaces specified for the purpose along with all general information sought for the same;

x. They were requested to complete the assignment within an hour.

xi. The answer sheets were collected from the students at a time by giving a bell.

4.2. SCORING OF THE SCALE

SCORING OF THE EMOTIONAL MATURITY SCALE (EMS-$_{SB}$)

The answered booklet containing the responses made by the students by then collected and scored according to the manual. Items of the scale are in question form demanding information for each in any of the five options. The items are so stated that if the answer is very much a score of 5 is given; for much 4; for undecided 3; and for probably 2 and for negative answer of never a score of 1 is to be awarded. Therefore, total score on the scale is indicative of emotional maturity whereas the greater the total score on the scale is expressed in terms of emotional immaturity.

4.3. STUDY OF SCORE DISTRIBUTION

The scores were compiled and put into a frequency distribution in order to calculate the measures of central tendencies and variations. The mean and variances of total samples as well as sub samples were calculated. Then categorization was made accordingly and the mean and standard deviation according to these variables were grouped together. These had been presented in the following terms:

4.4. DISTRIBUTION OF SCORES ON EMOTIONAL MATURITY SCALE

The scores of Emotional Maturity of College Students were tabulated and scores of the sample were given as follows according to the scores of sub-samples that were boys and girls. The Emotional Maturity of College Students was compiled and the highest and the lowest scores were found.

The scores ranged from 57-171 in case of male, 61-176 in case of female, and 57-176 in case of total. The distribution of scores of Emotional Maturity of the entire sample was given below in the table:

Table 4: Frequency distribution of the total sample, male and female on Emotional Maturity

Class - Interval	Frequencies		
	Total	Male	Female
170 – 179	2	1	1
160 – 169	3	2	1
150 – 159	4	2	2
140 – 149	8	5	3
130 – 139	10	5	5
120 – 129	12	6	6
110 – 119	14	8	6
100 – 109	13	7	6
90 – 99	11	6	5
80 – 89	9	4	5
70 – 79	7	3	4
60 – 69	5	1	4
50 – 59	2	0	2
Total	100	50	50

From the above table it was quite evident that the higher ranges of score had been displayed in case of female sub sample. In both cases, class interval 110 – 119 was considered as the modal class interval and gradually tapering towards the upper and lower end. It was observed in both sub samples. Such a distribution gave an impression of scores falling into a normal distribution.

4.5. Study of Normality on the Scores of Emotional Maturity of College Students

In order to study the normality in distribution of scores on emotional maturity of college students, the descriptive measures of Mean, Median, Mode, Standard Deviation, Quartile, and Percentile of scores on emotional maturity scale were calculated and presented in table.

Table 5: Descriptive Measures on Emotional Maturity of College Students Scores of the Total Sample

Variation		N	Mean	Median	Mode	SD	P_{90}	P_{10}	Q_3	Q_1	Q
Gender	Male	50	109.46	110	126	30.36	140	90	130.63	99.37	115
	Female	50	116.56	113.5	118	29.46	141.66	75	129.17	87.5	108.34
Total		100	113	110.5	126	29.97	140.71	83.6	130	94.29	112.14

From the above given table it was inferred that sample mean, median, mode are found to be 113, 110.5 and 126 respectively. The semi-inter quartile range of the distribution of scores being 112.14, the sum of the median and semi-quartile range was found to be 222.64 and the difference between the two was 1.64. The third and first quartiles of the distribution were 130 and 94.29 respectively.

If the sum and difference between the median and the semi-interquartile range became the same with the third and the first quartile respectively than they gave the evidence towards normality in distribution of scores on emotional maturity scale. As in the above given case, it was approximately the same, hence it was inferred that the distribution was normal distribution. The distribution of emotional maturity scores had been studied by plotting the scores as per the normal distribution. The result indicated that the mean, median, and mode of the distribution did not coincide and the distribution was both influenced by Skewness and Kurtosis. The Skewness of the normal probability curve was 0.17 as against 0 in case of normal value and kurtosis was found to be -0.89 as against the normal value of 0.263. This indicated that the distribution of scores from normality stand point was positively skewed and Platokurtic but the magnitude of difference was very high. Considering the result investigation was mentioned to conclude that the result obtained due to investigation was almost normal bearing aside the slight abnormality due to sampling error. This could be better understood with the help of the following figures. The frequencies and smoothed frequencies had been plotted into a frequency polygon curve with the smoothed frequency polygon superimposed on it. The Ogive had also been drawn for both male and female and the total on emotional maturity scores.

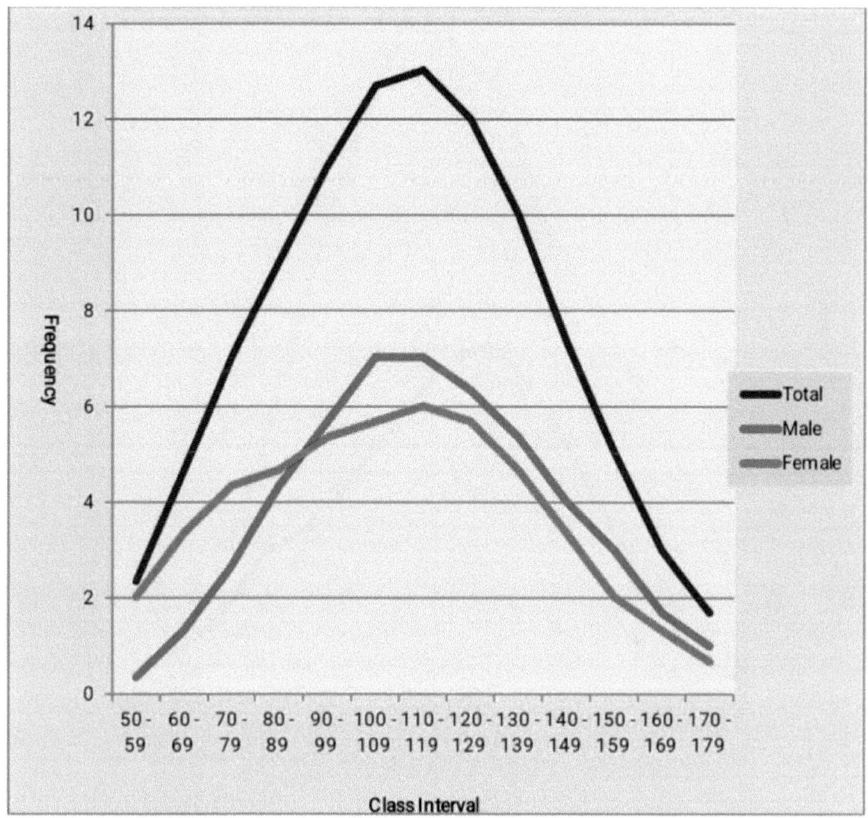

Figure:(iii) Frequency Polygon Showing the Emotional Maturity of College Students in Relation to Gender Difference

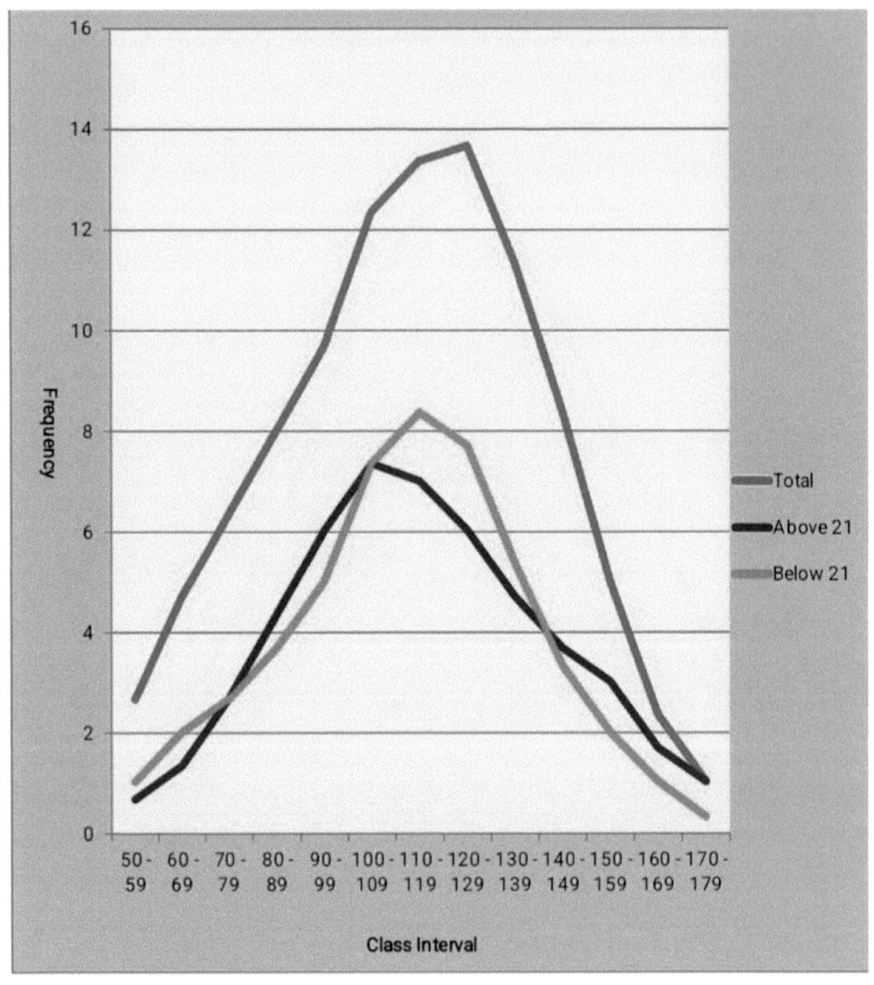

Figure: (iv) Frequency Polygon showing Emotional Maturity of college students in relation to Age Variation (total sample)

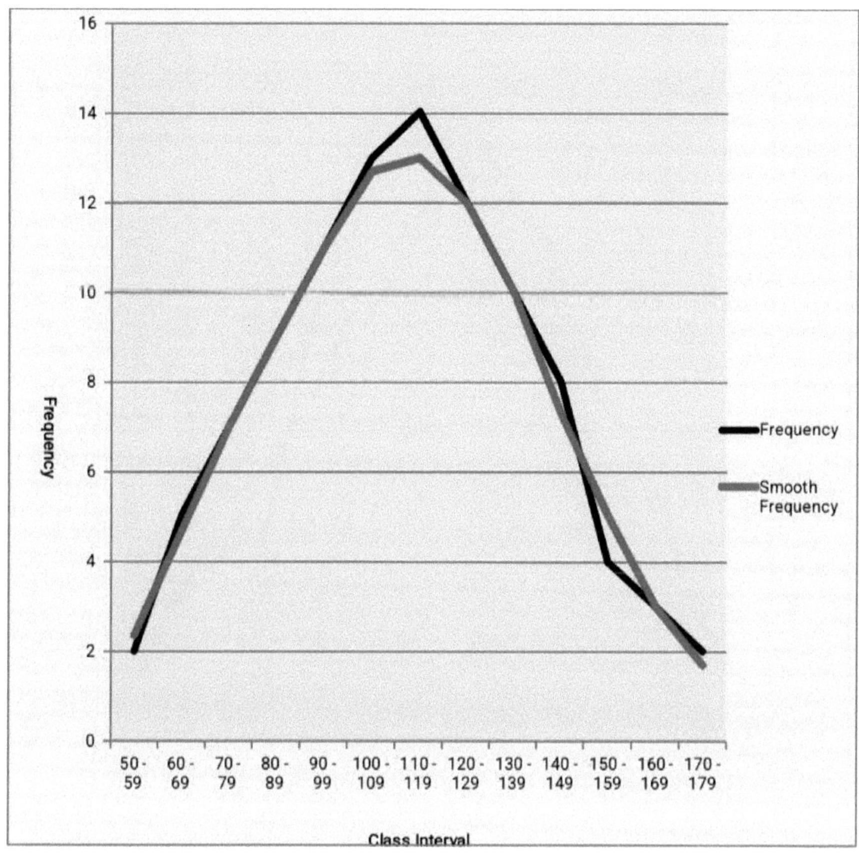

Figure:(v) Frequency Polygon with Smoothed Frequency superimposed of Emotional Maturity of College Students on Total Scores

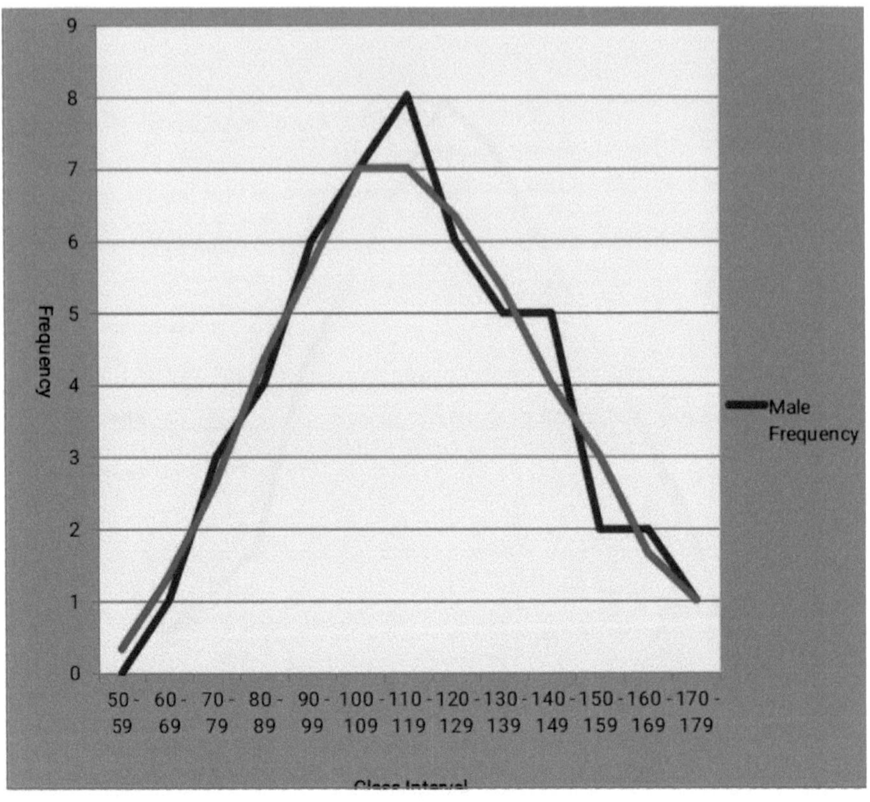

Figure: (vi) Normal Probability Curve with Smoothed Frequency superimposed of sub-sample (Male) on Emotional Maturity Scores

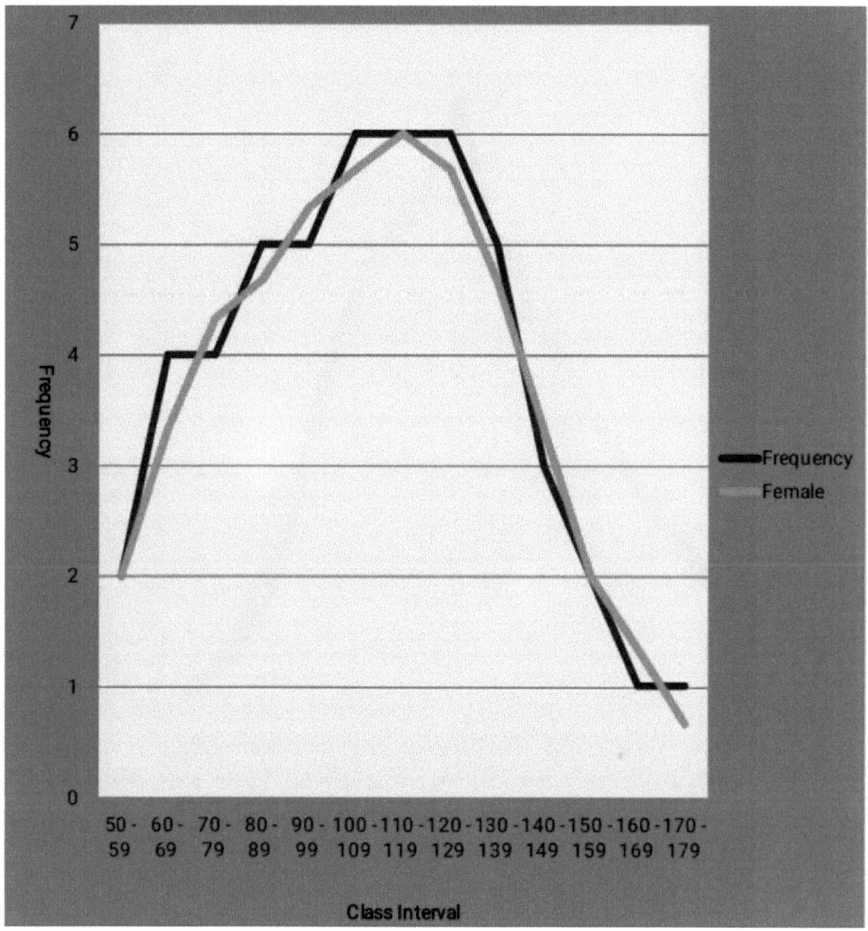

Figure:(vii) Normal Probability Curve with Smoothed Frequency superimposed of sub-sample (Female) on Emotional Maturity Scores

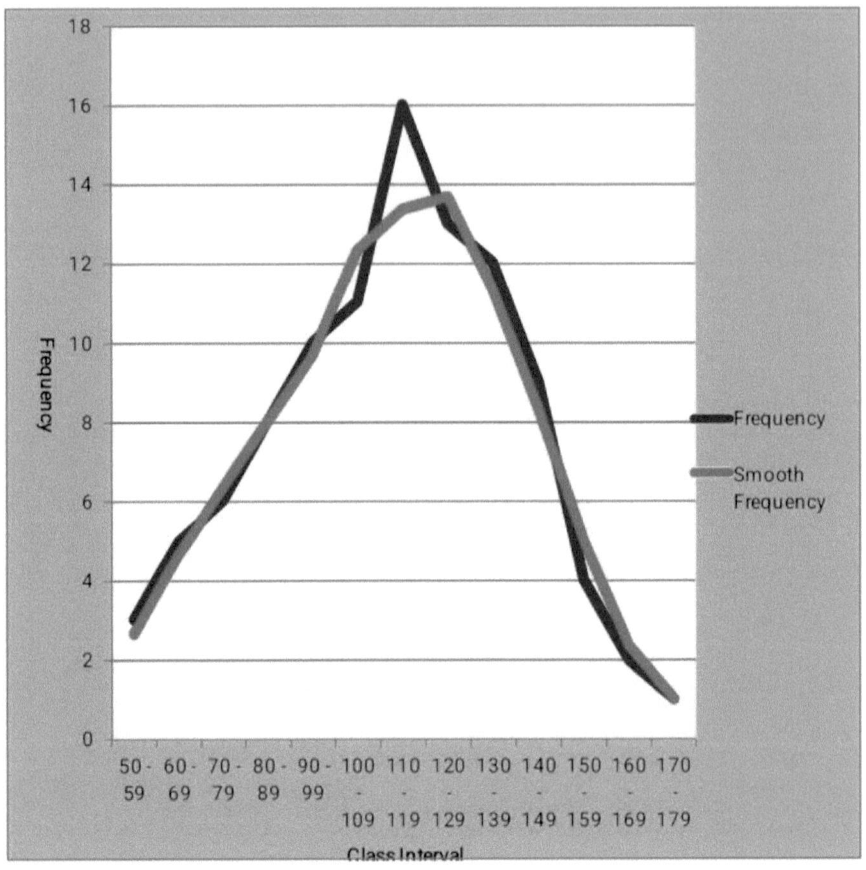

Figure: (viii) Normal Probability Curve with Smoothed Frequency superimposed of sub-sample (Age Above 21) on Emotional Maturity Scores

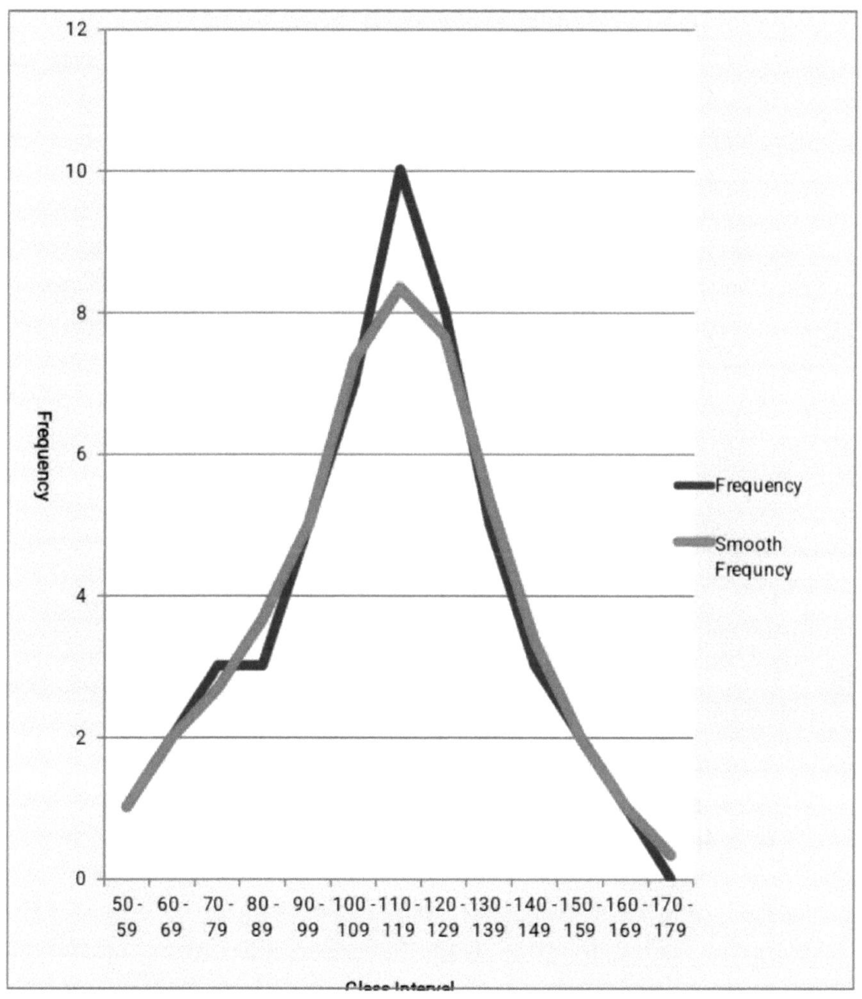

Figure: (ix) Normal Probability Curve with Smoothed Frequency superimposed of sub-sample (Age Below 21) on Emotional Maturity Scores

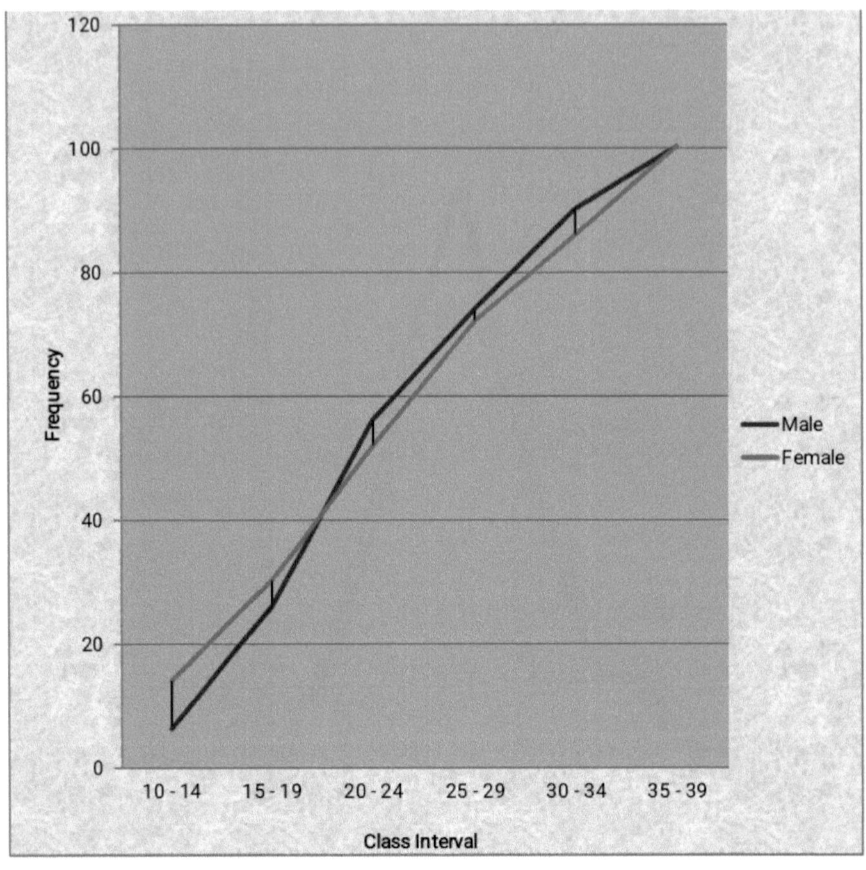

Figure:(x) Ogive for the Total Sample (Male And Female) on Emotional Stability scores

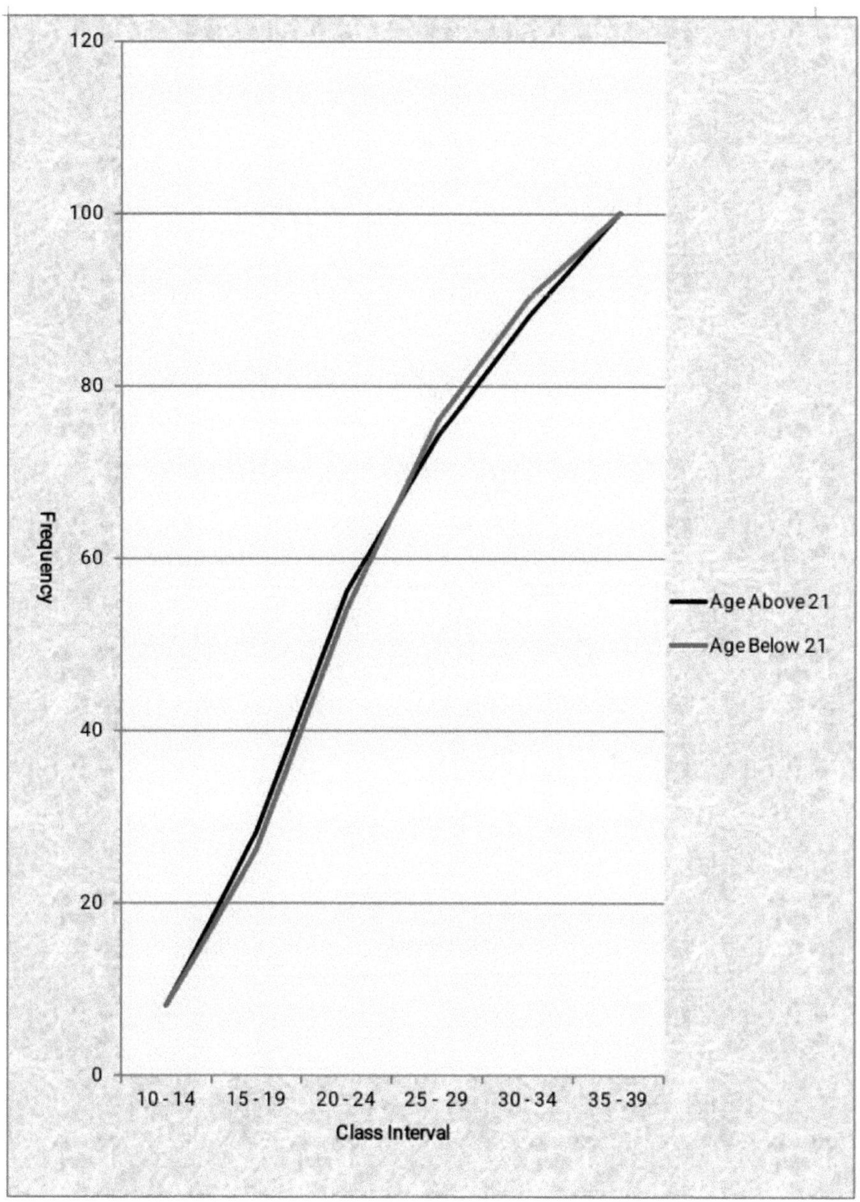

Figure:(xi) Ogive for the Total Sample (Age above 21 and below 21) on Emotional Stability scores

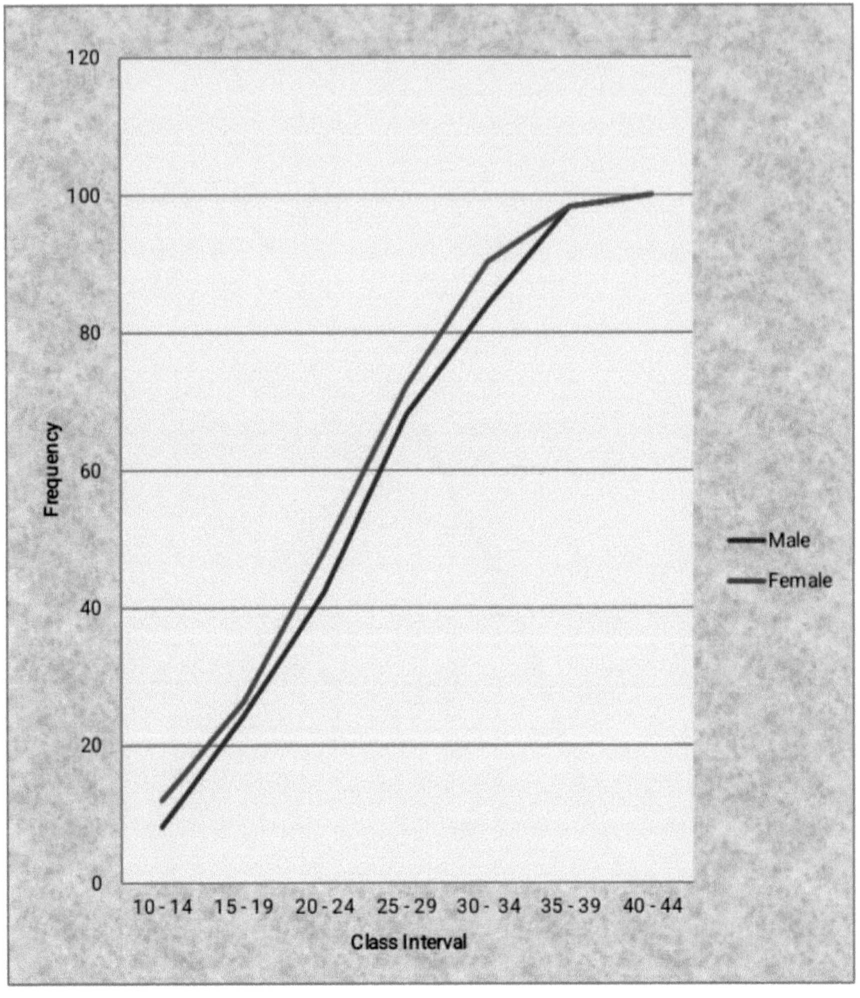

Figure:(xii) Ogive for the total sample (Male and Female) on Emotional Progression Scores

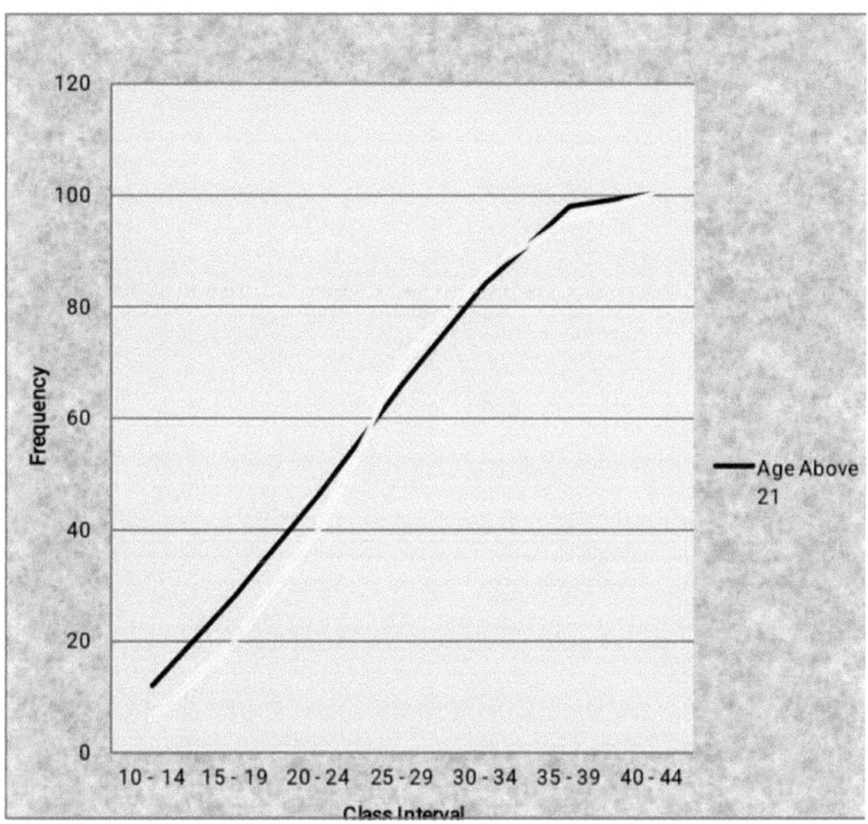

Figure:(xiii) Ogive for the total sample (Age above 21 and below 21) on Emotional Progression scores

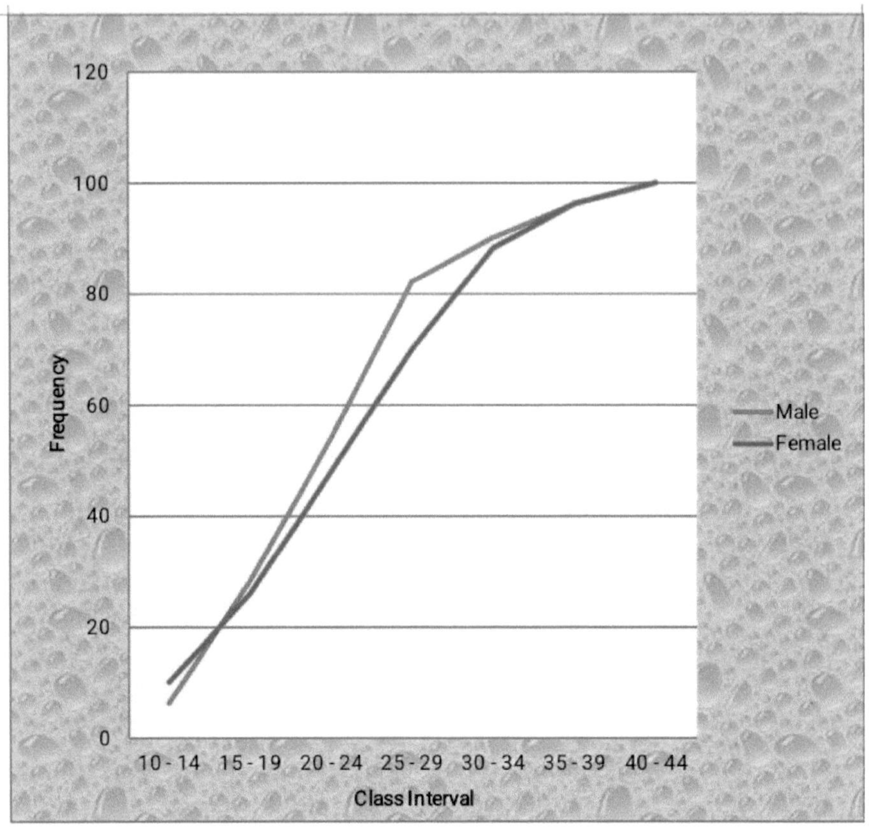

Figure: (xiv) Ogive for the total sample (Male and Female) on Social Adjustment Scores

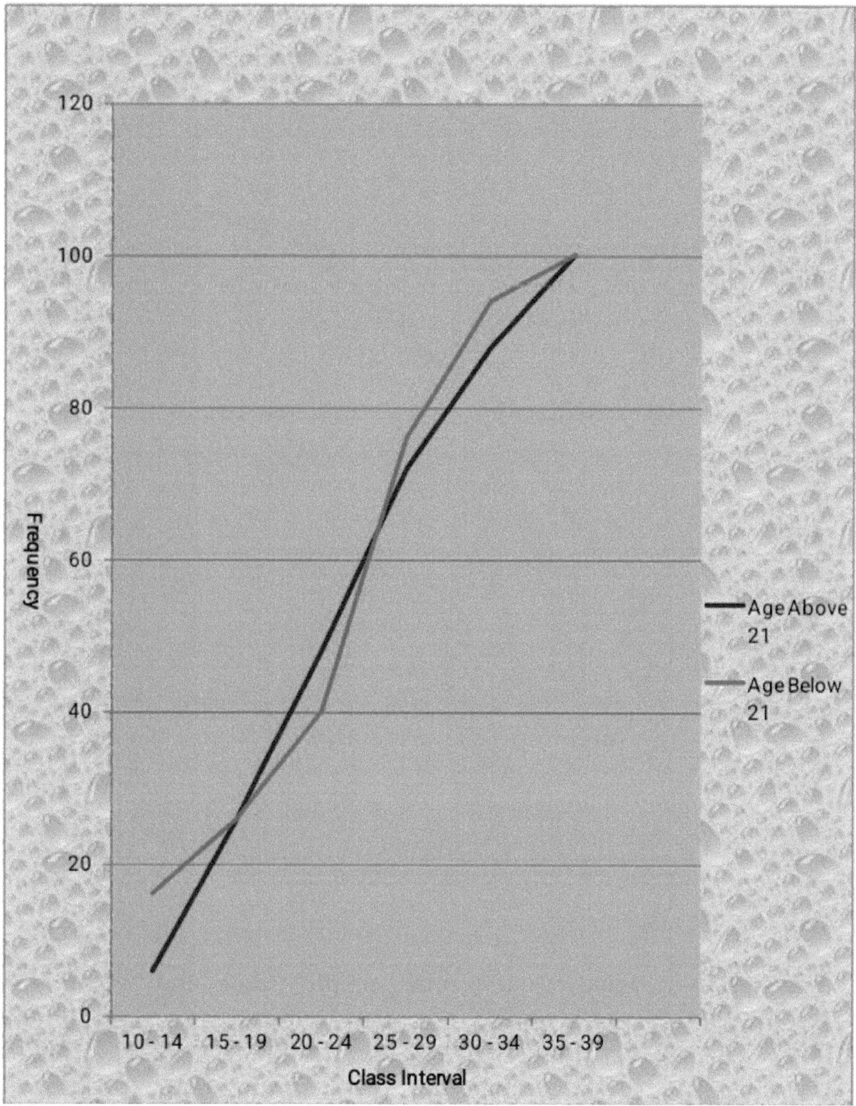

Figure:(xv) Ogive for the total sample (Age above 21 and below 21) on Social Adjustment scores

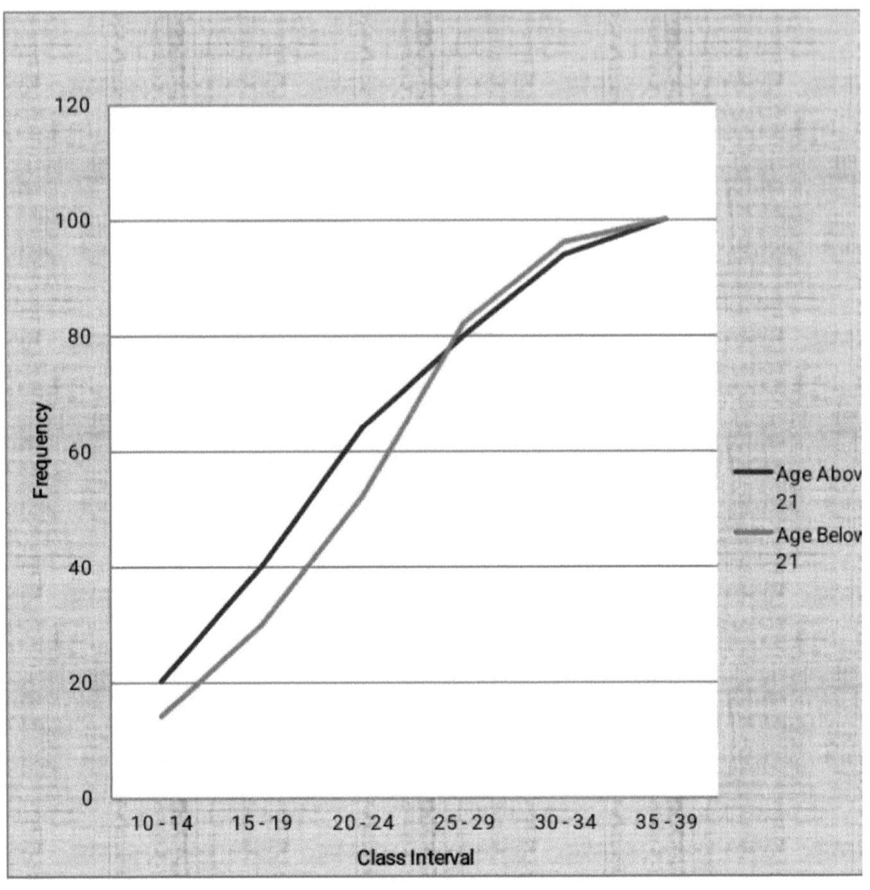

Figure: (xvi) Ogive for the total sample (Male and Female) on Personality Integration score

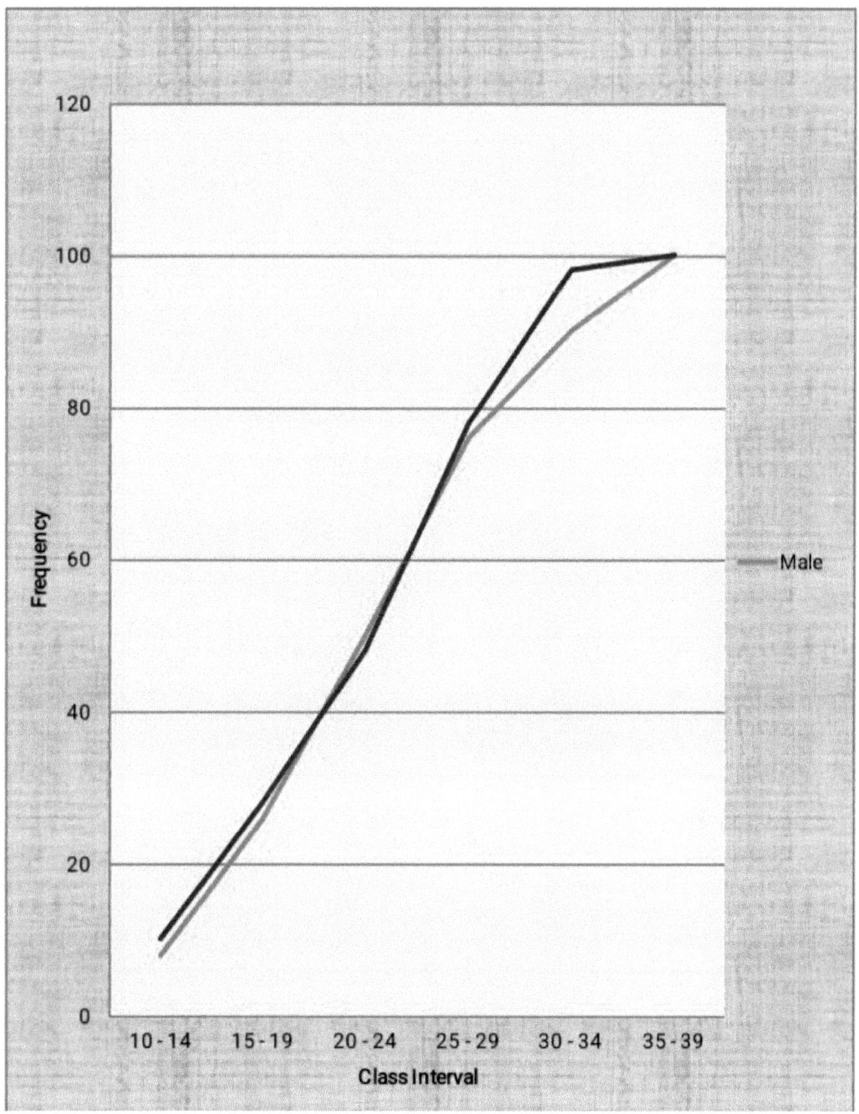

Figure:(xvii) Ogive for the total sample (Age above 21 and below 21) on Personality Integration scores

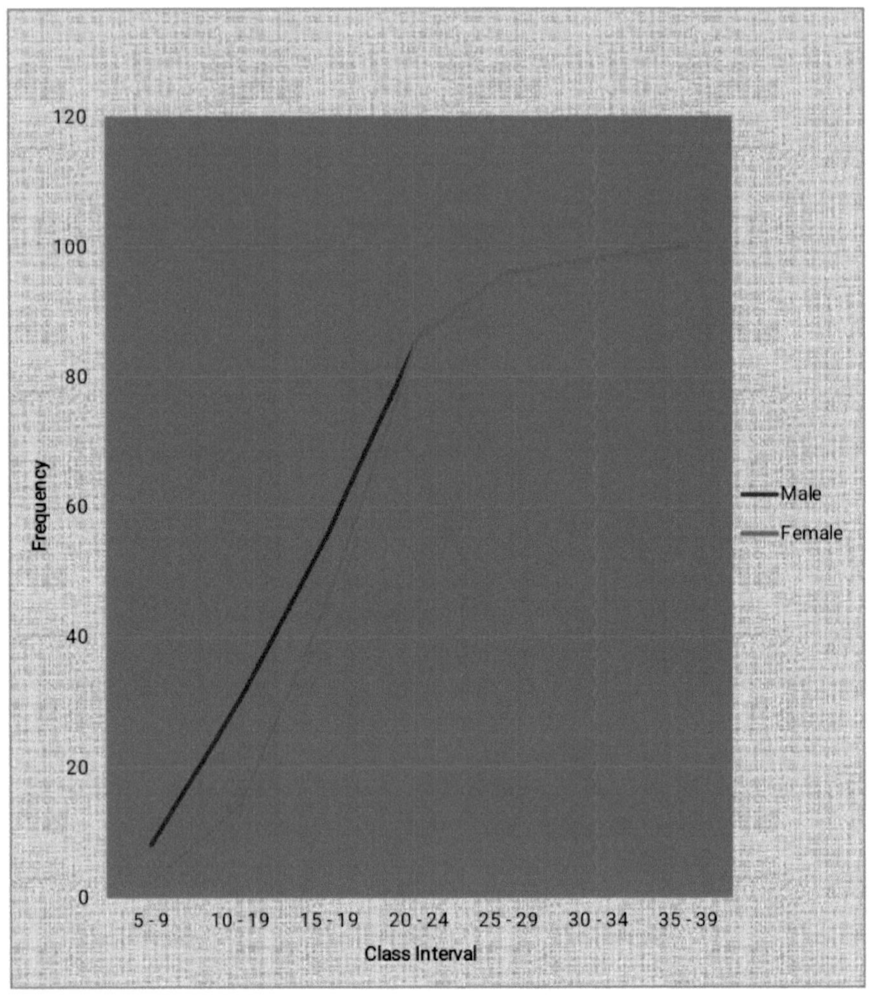

Figure:(xviii) Ogive for the Total Sample (Male and Female) on Independence scores

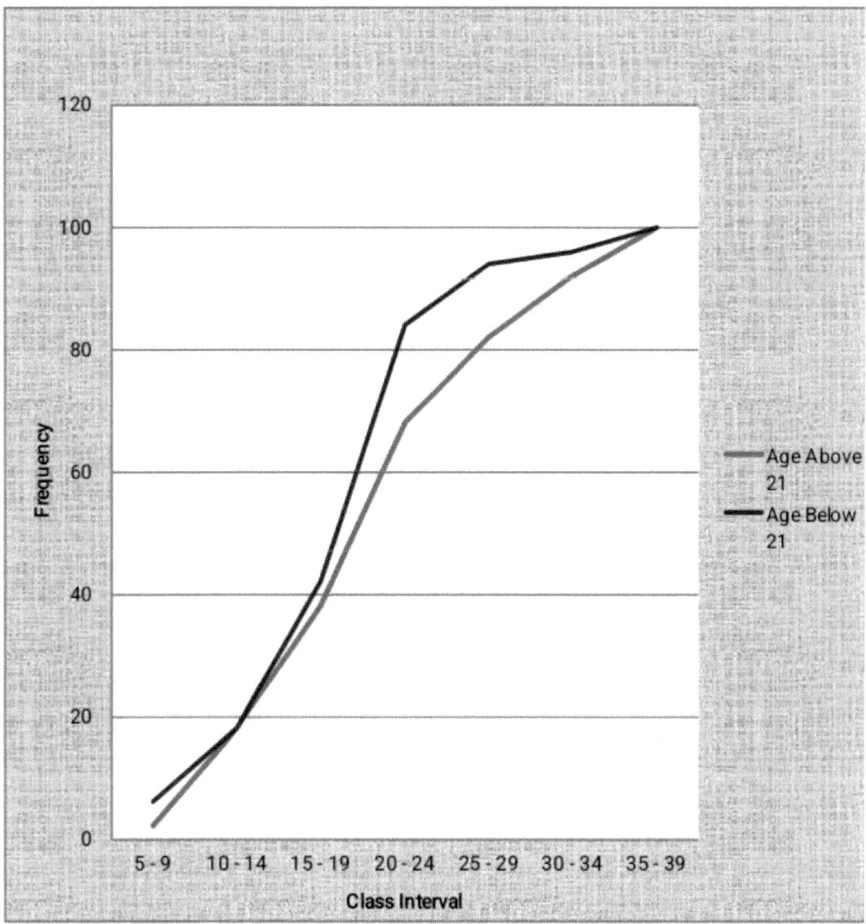

Figure:(xix) Ogive for the Total Sample (Age above 21 and below 21) on Independence scores

CHAPTER FIVE

ANALYSIS AND INTERPRETATION OF DATA

In the first and second chapter a vivid description of the problem context had been outlined along with the problem focus by citing instances from different reviews of related researches. The third chapter was devoted to elaborate the design and procedure adopted for the study, the development of emotional maturity scale was discussed in the fourth chapter whereas the first part of the fifth chapter was devoted to organization and collection of data according to the objective and hypotheses formulated in the second chapter. In the second part of this chapter it was intended to present an analysis of the results that had been obtained through the application of the method and procedure mentioned earlier. The results were presented in the tables followed by discussion. The findings were collaborated with earlier researches for confirmation of the results by including these variables. The results were organized under differential analysis and study relationship on the variables and between the variables.

5.1 HYPOTHESES TESTING

Under this subsection attempts were made by the investigator to interpret the data in terms of the objectives and hypotheses formulated earlier. For this the sample was split into two sub-samples namely:

- Male Vs Female
- Age Above 21years Vs Age Below 21years

In order to make a statistical comparison the 't' ratios were calculated in all the cases and the results were presented in each and every cases. For determining the significance of difference between the means and variances of each of the contrasts the 't' ratios were calculated and tested for significance at 0.05 level and 0.01 level of significance and depending upon the result, the hypotheses were rejected or accepted. The corroboration of earlier studies was made with regard to the result and interpretation was made accordingly. The details of this were presented in tables in the following pages.

5.2 ANALYSIS OF THE TOTAL SAMPLE IN RELATION TO GENDER AND AGE VARIATIONS

5.2.1 Analysis of Emotional Maturity of College Students in Relation to Gender Variation (In Total)

In order to test to test the gender difference in emotional maturity (in total) of college students 't' ratio had been calculated and presented below:

Table 6: Test of significance of difference on Emotional Maturity of college students (in total) due to gender variation

Variation	Sub Sample	N	M	SD	SE_D	'T'	Remark
Gender	Male	50	109.46	30.36	5.98	1.18	NS
	Female	50	116.56	29.45			

P values of t at 0.05 level= 1.98, 0.01 level= 2.63 for df 98, NS refers to Not Significant

It was quite evident from the above table that the obtained value of 't' ratio was 1.18 which was smaller than the table value 0.05 level= 1.98, 0.01 level= 2.63. Hence the't' ratio (1.18) in case of gender variation was not significant at 0.05 and 0.01 level and we may concluded that there was no significant difference between male and female in their emotional maturity.

The result was in the conformity with the earlier studies done by **Sivakumar(2010), Wani& Masih (2015) , Gakher (2003), Meenakshi & Saurashtra (2003) and Kour (2001)**, which found there is no significant difference between males and females on emotional maturity.

5.2.2 Analysis of Emotional Maturity of College Students in Relation to Age Variation (Total)

In order to test to test the age difference in emotional maturity (total) of college students 't' ratio had been calculated and presented below:

Table 7: Test of significance of difference on Emotional Maturity of college students (total) due to Age variation

Variation	Sub Sample	N	M	SD	SE_D	'T'	Remark
Age	Above 21	50	116.52	31.04	5.98	1.17	NS
	Below 21	50	109.5	28.75			

P values of t at 0.05 level= 1.98, 0.01 level= 2.63 for d f 98, NS refers to Not Significant

It was quite evident from the above table that the obtained value of 't' ratio was 1.17 which was smaller than the table value 0.05 level= 1.98, 0.01 level= 2.63. Hence the 't' ratio (1.17) in case of age variation was not significant at 0.05 and 0.01 level and we may concluded that there was no significant difference in their emotional maturity due to age difference. The result was in the conformity with the earlier studies done by Louis and Doss (2007) & Lichtenberg (2005). They also found that there does not exist any difference due to age variation.

5.3 ANALYSIS OF THE TOTAL SAMPLE SUB-SAMPLE WISE

5.3.1 Analysis of Emotional Stability of College Students in Relation to Gender Variation

One of the objectives of the study was to estimate the Emotional Stability of college students in relation to gender variation. For this the null hypothesis HO_1 was formulated as follows, "There will be no significant difference in the emotional stability of college students in relation to gender variation". In order to test the gender difference in emotional stability of college students 't' ratio had been calculated and presented below:

Table 8: Test of significance of difference on Emotional Stability of college students due to gender variation

Variation	Sub Sample	N	M	SD	SE_D	'T'	Remark
Gender	Male	50	23.38	7.58			NS
	Female	50	25.42	7.50	1.51	1.35	

P values of t at 0.05 level= 1.98, 0.01 level= 2.63 for df 98, NS refers to Not Significant

It was quite evident from the above table that the obtained value of 't' ratio was 1.35 which was smaller than the table value 0.05 level= 1.98, 0.01 level= 2.63. Hence the't' ratio (1.35) in case of gender variation was not significant at 0.05 and 0.01 level. So the null hypothesis HO_1 "there will be no significant difference in the emotional stability of college students in relation to gender variation" could not be rejected and concluded that there was no significant difference between male and female in their emotional stability.

5.3.2 Analysis of Emotional Stability of College Students in Relation to Age Variation

One of the objectives of the study was to estimate the Emotional Stability of college students in relation to age variation. For this the null hypothesis HO_2 was formulated as follows "There will be no significant difference in the emotional stability of college students in relation to age variation". For the appropriateness of the study, 't' ratio was calculated as shown in the following table.

Table 9: Test of significance of difference on Emotional Stability of college students due to age variation

Variation	Sub Sample	N	M	SD	SE_D	'T'	Remark
Age	Above 21	50	24.86	7.27	1.52	0.61	NS
	Below 21	50	23.94	7.91			

P values of t at 0.05 level= 1.98, 0.01 level= 2.63 for df 98, NS refers to Not Significant

On the above given data it was quite evident that the obtained value of 't' ratio was 0.61 and less than table value which is 1.98 at 0.05 level and 2.63 at 0.01 level of significance. Hence the 't' ratio could not be significant. So the null hypothesis Ho_2 "there will be no significant difference in the emotional stability of college students in relation to age variation" could not be rejected and it was concluded that there was no significant difference between students having age above 21 and below 21 on their emotional stability.

5.3.3 Analysis of Emotional Progression of College Students in Relation to Gender Variation

One of the objectives of the study was to estimate the Emotional Progression of college students in relation to gender variation. For this the null hypothesis Ho_3 was formulated as follows,"There will be no significant difference in the emotional progression of college students in relation to gender variation". For the appropriateness of the study and in order to test the differences in emotional progression the 't' ratio was calculated as shown in the following table.

Table 10: Test of significance of difference on Emotional Progression of college students due to Gender variation

Variation	Sub Sample	N	M	SD	SE_D	'T'	Remark
Gender	Male	50	23.12	7.28			
	Female	50	25.36	8.12	1.54	1.45	NS

P values of t at 0.05 level= 1.98, 0.01 level= 2.63 for df 98, NS refers to Not Significant

On the above given data it was quite evident that the obtained value of 't' ratio was 1.45 and less than table value which is 1.98 at 0.05 level and 2.63 at 0.01 level of significance. Hence the 't' ratio could not be significant. So the null hypothesis Ho_2 "there will be no significant difference in the emotional progression of college students in relation to gender variation" could not be rejected and it was concluded that there was no significant difference between male and female students in their emotion progression.

5.3.4 Analysis of Emotional Progression of College Students in Relation to Age Variation

One of the objectives of the study was to estimate the Emotional Progression of college students in relation to age variation. For this the null hypothesis Ho4 was formulated as follows, “there will be no significant difference in the emotional progression of college students in relation to age variation”. For the appropriateness of the study and in order to test the age differences in emotional progression,‘t’ ratio was calculated as shown in the following table.

Table 11: Test of significance of difference on Emotional Progression of college students due to Age variation

Variation	Sub Sample	N	M	SD	SE_D	'T'	Remark
Age	Above 21	50	25.08	8.22	1.54	1.09	NS
	Above 21	50	23.4	7.23			

P values of t at 0.05 level= 1.98, 0.01 level= 2.63 for df 98, NS refers to Not Significant

On the above given data it was quite evident that the obtained value of ‘t’ ratio was 1.09 and less than table value which is 1.98 at 0.05 level and 2.63 at 0.01 level of significance. Hence the ‘t’ ratio could not be significant. So the null hypothesis Ho_4 “there will be no significant difference in the emotional progression of college students in relation to age variation” could not be rejected and it was concluded that there was no significant difference between students in their emotion progression due to difference in age.

5.3.5 Analysis of Social Adjustment of College Students in Relation to Gender Variation

One of the objectives of the study was to estimate the Social Adjustmentof college students in relation to gender variation. For this the null hypothesis Ho_5 There will be no significant difference in the social adjustment of college students in relation to gender variation. For the appropriateness of the study and in order to test the differences in social adjustment the‘t’ ratio was calculated as shown in the following table.

Table 12: Test of significance of difference on Social Adjustment of college students due to Gender variation

Variation	Sub Sample	N	M	SD	SED	'T'	Remark
Gender	Male	50	22.92	7.50			
	Female	50	23.5	6.84	1.44	0.40	NS

P values of t at 0.05 level= 1.98, 0.01 level= 2.63 for df 98, NS refers to Not Significant

On the above given data it was quite evident that the obtained value of 't' ratio was 0.40 and less than table value which is 1.98 at 0.05 level and 2.63 at 0.01 level of significance. Hence the 't' ratio(0.04) could not be significant. So the null hypothesis Ho_5 "there will be no significant difference in the social adjustment of college students in relation to gender variation" could not be rejected and it was concluded that there was no significant difference between male and female students in their social adjustment.

5.3.6 Analysis of Social Adjustment of College Students in Relation to Age Variation

One of the objectives of the study was to estimate the social adjustment of college students in relation to age variation. For this the null hypothesis Ho_6 There will be no significant difference in the social adjustment of college students in relation to age variation. For the appropriateness of the study and in order to test the age differences in social adjustment, 't' ratio was calculated as shown in the following table.

Table 13: Test of significance of difference on Social Adjustment of college students due to Age variation

Variation	Sub Sample	N	M	SD	SED	't'	Remark
Age	Above 21	50	24.78	7.42			
	Above 21	50	21.64	6.56	1.40	2.24	S

P values of t at 0.05 level= 1.98, 0.01 level= 2.63 for df 98, S refers to Significant

On the above given data it was quite evident that the obtained value of ‘t’ ratio was 2.24 which was greater than table value which is 1.98 at 0.05 level but lesser than 2.63 at 0.01 level of significance. Hence the ‘t’ ratio(2.24) in case of age variation was significant at 0.05 level. So the null hypothesis Ho_6 “there will be no significant difference in the social adjustment of college students in relation to age variation” could be rejected and it was concluded that there was significant difference between students in their social adjustment due to difference in age.

The result was in the conformity of the research conducted by **Sharma (2012).** He also found that there is a difference between first year and final year students in social adjustments. **Sinha (2014)& Mahmoudi (2012)** also found a high correlation between this age variation and social and any other adjustment.

5.3.7 Analysis of Personality Integration of College Students in Relation to Gender Variation

One of the objectives of the study was to estimate the Personality Integrationof college students in relation to gender variation. For this the null hypothesis Ho_7 “There will be no significant difference in the personality integration of college students in relation to gender variation”. For the appropriateness of the study and in order to test the differences in social adjustment the‘t’ ratio was calculated as shown in the following table.

Table 14: Test of significance of difference on Personality Integration of college students due to Gender variation

Variation	Sub Sample	N	M	SD	SE_D	‘t’	Remark
Gender	Male	50	21.14	8.46	1.62	1.04	NS
	Female	50	22.82	7.72			

P values of t at 0.05 level= 1.98, 0.01 level= 2.63 for df 98, NS refers to Not Significant

On the above given data it was quite evident that the obtained value of ‘t’ ratio was 1.04 and less than table value which is 1.98 at 0.05 level and 2.63 at 0.01 level of significance. Hence the ‘t’ ratio(1.04) could not be significant. So the null hypothesis Ho7“There will be no significant difference in the personality integration of college students in relation to gender variation" could not be rejected and it was concluded that there was no significant difference between male and female students in their personality integration.

5.3.8 Analysis of Personality Integration of College Students in Relation to Age Variation

One of the objectives of the study was to estimate the personality integration of college students in relation to age variation. For this the null hypothesis Ho_8 There will be no significant difference in the personality integration of college students in relation to age variation. For the appropriateness of the study and in order to test the age differences in social adjustment, 't' ratio was calculated as shown in the following table.

Table 15: Test of significance of difference on Personality Integration of college students due to Age variation

Variation	Sub Sample	N	M	SD	SE_D	't'	Remark
Age	Above 21	50	23.14	8.51	1.61	1.44	NS
	Above 21	50	20.82	7.57			

P values of t at 0.05 level= 1.98, 0.01 level= 2.63 for df 98, N S refers to Not Significant

On the above given data it was quite evident that the obtained value of 't' ratio was 1.44 which was lesser than table value which is 1.98 at 0.05 level and 2.63 at 0.01 level of significance. Hence the 't' ratio(1.44) in case of age variation was not significant. So the null hypothesis Ho_8 "there will be no significant difference in the personality integration of college students in relation to age variation" could not be rejected and it was concluded that there was no significant difference between students in their personality integration due to difference in age.

5.3.9 Analysis of Independence of College Students in Relation to Gender Variation

One of the objectives of the study was to estimate the Independenceof college students in relation to gender variation. For this the null hypothesis Ho_9 "There will be no significant difference in the independence of college students in relation to gender variation". For the appropriateness of the study and in order to test the differences in social adjustment the't' ratio was calculated as shown in the following table.

Table 16: Test of significance of difference on Independence of college students due to Gender variation

Variation	Sub Sample	N	M	SD	SE_D	't"	Remark
Gender	Male	50	18.9	6.22			
	Female	50	19.46	4.55	1.08	0.52	NS

P values of t at 0.05 level= 1.98, 0.01 level= 2.63 for df 98, NS refers to Not Significant

On the above given data it was quite evident that the obtained value of 't' ratio was 0.52 and less than table value which is 1.98 at 0.05 level and 2.63 at 0.01 level of significance. Hence the 't' ratio(0.52) could not be significant. So the null hypothesis Ho_9 "There will be no significant difference in the independence of college students in relation to gender variation" could not be rejected and it was concluded that there was no significant difference between male and female students in their independence.

5.3.10 Analysis of Independence of College Students in Relation to Age Variation

One of the objectives of the study was to estimate the independence of college students in relation to age variation. For this the null hypothesis Ho_{10} There will be no significant difference in the independence of college students in relation to age variation. For the appropriateness of the study and in order to test the age differences in independence, 't' ratio was calculated as shown in the following table.

Table 17: Test of significance of difference on Independence of college students due to Age variation

Variation	Sub Sample	N	M	SD	SE_D	't'	Remark
Age	Above 21	50	18.66	5.19	1.08	0.96	NS
	Above 21	50	19.7	5.67			

P values of t at 0.05 level= 1.98, 0.01 level= 2.63 for df 98, N S refers to Not Significant

On the above given data it was quite evident that the obtained value of 't' ratio was 0.96 which was lesser than table value which is 1.98 at 0.05 level and 2.63 at 0.01 level of significance. Hence the 't' ratio(0.96) in case of age variation was not significant. So the null hypothesis Ho_{10} "there will be no significant difference in the independence of college students in relation to age variation" could not be rejected and it was concluded that there was no significant difference between students in their independence due to difference in age.

CHAPTER SIX

SUMMARY AND RECOMMENDATION

6.1 THE SUMMARY

Emotional maturity is defined as, "A process in which the personality is continually striving for greater sense of emotional health, both intra-psychically and intra-personally". In brief emotional maturity can be called as the process of impulse control through the agency of "self" or "ego".

Emotional maturity is not only the effective determinant of personality pattern but it also helps to control the growth of adolescent's development. The concept "Mature" emotional behavior of any level is that which reflects the fruits of normal emotional development. A person who is able to keep his emotions under control i.e., able to break delay and to suffer without self-pity, might still be emotionally stunned and childish. Morgan (1934) stated the view that an adequate theory of emotional maturity must take account of the full scope of the individuality, power and his ability to enjoy the use of his powers. According to Walter D Smithson (1974) emotional maturity is a process in which the personality is continuously striving for greater sense of emotional health, both intra-psychically and intra-personality.

Kaplan and Baron elaborate the characteristics of an emotionally mature person; say that he has the capacity to withstand delay in satisfaction of needs. He has the ability to tolerate a reasonable amount of frustration. He has belief in long-term planning and is capable of delaying or revising his expectations in terms of demands of situations. An emotionally mature child has the capacity to make effective adjustment with himself, members of his family his peers in the school, society and culture. But maturity means not merely the capacity for such attitude and functioning but also the ability to enjoy them fully.

L.S Hollingsworth (1928) mentions some characteristics of emotionally mature person in the following points-

i. He is capable of responding in gradation or degree of emotional responses. He does not respond in all or none fashion, but keeps within bounds. If his hat blows off, he does not blow up.
ii. He is also able to delay his responses as controlled with the impulsiveness of young child.
iii. Handling of self pity, instead of showing unrestrained self pity, he tries to feel for him.

Childhood emotional stresses influence the infant's congenital heredity plus physical and emotional forces acting upon sperm and egg, (prior to conception and until birth) endowment and development forces, the child being most formative up to the age of about six.

The most outstanding mark of emotional maturity, accordance to Cole (1944) is ability to bear tension. Other marks are an indifference toward certain kinds of stimuli that affect the child o adolescent and he develops moodiness and sentimentally. Besides, emotionally matured person persist the capacity for fun and recreation. He enjoys both play and responsibility activities and keep them in proper balance.

According to Fred McKinney, "The characteristics of an emotionally mature are hetero-sexuality, appreciation of attitude and behavior of others, tendency to adopt the attitudes and habits of others and capacity to delay his own responses."Therefore, the emotionally mature is not one who necessarily has resolved all conditions that aroused anxiety and hostility but it is continuously in process of seeing himself in clear perspective, continually involved in a struggle to gain healthy integration of feeling, thinking action.

RATIONALE OF THE STUDY

In the present circumstances, youth as well as children are facing difficulties in life. These difficulties are giving rise to many psycho-somatic problems such as anxiety, tensions, frustrations and emotional upsets in day to day life. So the study of emotional life is now emerging as a descriptive science, comparable with anatomy. It deals with interplay of forces with intensities and quantities. Available tests are crude and measure chiefly the degree of dependence. But this test measures the different aspects of emotional maturity. As self acceptance is an important aspect of maturity says Wenkart, and it must be preceded by acceptance from others.

The specific needs for identifying these phenomena of Emotional Maturity as a natural and inevitable essential outcome of student growth and development rather than among pathological symptom. The Emotional maturity becomes important in the behavior of individuals. As the students are the pillars of the future generations their value pattern of Emotional Maturity are vital. So the present study intends to measure the Emotional Maturity of college students. While doing the research, the researcher tried to answer the following queries.

- Are the college students emotionally stable in relation to gender and age variation?
- Are the college students emotionally progressed in relation to gender and age variation?
- Are the college students socially adjusted in relation to gender and age variation?
- Do the college students have personality integration in relation to gender and age variation?
- Are the college students independent in relation to gender and age variation?

Objectives of the Study

- To study the emotional stability of college students in relation to gender and age variation.
- To study the emotional progression of college students in relation to gender and age variation.
- To study the social adjustment of college students in relation to gender and age variation.
- To study the personality integration of college students in relation to gender and age variation.
- To study the independence of college students in relation to gender and age variation.

Hypothesis of the Study

The null hypotheses for the research topic are as follows:

Ho_1: There is no significant difference in the emotional stability of college students in relation to gender variation.

Ho_2: There is no significant difference in the emotional stability of college students in relation to age variation.

Ho_3: There is no significant difference in the emotional progression of college students in relation to gender variation.

Ho_4: There is no significant difference in the emotional progression of college students in relation to age variation.

Ho_5: There is no significant difference in the social adjustment of college students in relation to gender variation.

Ho_6:There is no significant difference in the social adjustment of college students in relation to age variation.

Ho_7:There is no significant difference in the personality integration of college students in relation to gender variation.

Ho_8:There is no significant difference in the personality integration of college students in relation to age variation.

Ho_9: There is no significant difference in the independence of college students in relation to gender variation.

Ho_{10}: There is no significant difference in the independence of college students in relation to age variation.

OPERATIONAL DEFINITION

Emotional Maturity: Emotional Maturity is a process in which the personality is continuously striving for greater sense of emotional health, both intra-psychically and intra-personally (Singh and Bharagava, 2005).

College Students: It refers to the students studying in different government and private colleges.

SCOPE AND DELIMITATION OF THE STUDY

The scope of the study was to analyze the emotional maturity of college students of West Bengal. The study was delimited to 100 students selected from 4 colleges of West Bengal in a simple random basis.

METHODOLOGY

The Design

Normative survey method was adopted in the present research to obtain pertinent information concerning the area of the study. Hence, this method of ex-post facto type in nature and content was used in this study.

Sample

A sample of 100 students from 4 colleges of West Bengal was selected by simple random sampling procedure.

Tools used for the Study

Emotional Maturity Scale (EMS-$_{SB}$) developed by Singh and Bharagava (2005) was used for data collection. It consists of 48 items including several aspects of problems or issue related to emotional maturity.

Techniques of Data Analysis:

Various statistical techniques were used in the analysis of data as per the need of the data obtained. These techniques include descriptive as well as Inferential Statistics.

6.2 FINDINGS OF THE STUDY

- From the result it was found that most of the college students are emotionally immature. Findings also showed that there is no difference in emotional maturity in terms of gender variation.
- The distribution is normal distribution
- Age variation also did not play any vital role in the emotional maturity of the students. In many cases it was seen that being elder in age the students showed less emotional maturity.
- Male and female students having different age did not influence the emotional stability of college students.
- Male and female students having different age did not influence the emotional progression of college students.
- Gender variation did not play any vital role in case of social adjustment of college students.
- Age variation played a vital role in case of social adjustments of college students.
- Gender and age variation did not play any vital role in case of personality integration of college students.
- Gender and age variation did not play any vital role in case of independence of college students.

6.3 RECOMMENDATIONS

The present study highlights the level of emotional maturity among under graduate students across gender and age variation. It was found that majority of under graduates are emotionally unstable and also females are better emotionally then males. The under graduate students must try to understand that what lies there which make them emotionally unstable. The levels of education don't make them emotionally mature. Emotionally maturity is not something that grows with chronological age. Therefore they must decide to have emotionally maturity as a conscious choice and enjoy life in a happy and balanced way. Gender differences can be attributed to the variations in socialization process of both genders than to the inherent genetic character. Moreover, the difference is not so massive that it cannot be subdued.

Therefore the adults must be provided opportunities to strengthen their emotions so that they can easily face the realities of life and make successful adjustments.

6.4 EDUCATIONAL IMPLICATIONS OR IMPLICATION FOR FURTHER RESEARCH

There is always scope for further research in the same area. The present study was conducted on probability sampling of 100 students from different colleges. Study can be conducted on following problems:

- Study can be replicated on a large sample by including more districts so as present a clear picture of Emotional Maturity of college students in West Bengal.

- Similar studies can be conducted on Higher Secondary School, Universities etc.

The study focused on the emotional maturity of college students. The study can look at the maturity of college students. In this way the study confined to group of students at the under graduate level. Future research should be conducted on a bigger scale this will give more accurate data on the findings. Since present study is a pilot study the data was restricted to the four colleges of West Bengal. It would be interesting also if a similar study in the same area were to be conducted to compare the present finding with the student in other region in West Bengal. After the study of student's emotional maturity at college level in West Bengal the following measures are the recommendations for its improvement.

The present study may help the parents, teachers and administrators to have knowledge of the emotional development of their children and students and help them in building a well balanced personality. Emotional Development is one of the major aspects of human growth and development. Emotions like anger, fear, love etc. play a great role in the development of child's personality. Not only his physical growth and development is linked with his emotional makeup, but his intellectual, social, moral and aesthetic development are also controlled by his emotional behavior and experiences. The overall importance of emotional experiences in the life of a human being makes it quite essential to know about the emotions. Emotional development reaches its maximum in adulthood. During this stage, generally all individuals attain emotional maturity. The study will benefit the under graduates mainly and also post graduates and research scholars to have a kind attention towards their emotional development and will make them aware about the importance of emotional maturity in the present fast changing global world.

Bibliography

Aashra.B. , Jogsan.Y. *(2013)* Emotional Maturity and Self-Actualization in Graduate and Post-Graduate Students. *Quest Journals Journal of Research in Humanities and Social Science*

Aleem, S. (2005, july). "Emotional Stability among College Youth". *Journal of Indian Academy of Applied Psychology, 31*, 100-102.

Alka M. Mankad 1999 Personality Measurement of Emotionally Matured Adolescent Youth and Emotionally matured People, 5th International and 36th Indian Academy of Applied psychology Conference, Souvenir, December 27-29, 30.

Arya. A. (1984) "Emotional *maturity and value of superior children in family"*, Ph.D., Psychology, Agra University.

Best, J. W., & Kahn, J. V. (2010). Research in Education. New Delhi: PHI Learning Ltd.

Ferguson, G. A., & Yashio, T. (1989). Statistical Analysis in Psychology and Education. New York: McGraw Hill Book Co.

Festinger, L., & Katz, D. (1965). "Research Methods in the Behavioural Sciences", New York & New Delhi: Amerind Pub Co. Pvt Ltd & Holt, Rinehart & Winston New York, Indian Print.

Gupta and Poonam(2011) "*A comparative study between male and female adolescent school-going students on emotional maturity and achievement in co and curricular activities*". Ph.D. Education, Agra University, Rec Res Sci Tech 3 (2011) 153-155155

Hangal, S, & Aminabhavi, A. (2007) "*Self- Concept, Emotional Maturity and Achievement Motivation of the Adolescent Children of Employed Mothers and Homemakers*" Journal of Indian Academy of Applied Psychology, 33(1), 103-110.

Hussain, D. (2010) A Study of Parenting Style, Emotional Maturity and Academic Achievement among adolescents. Unpublished Ph.D Thesis, Jamia Millia Islamia, New Delhi. ISSN: 2026 – 6332 ©2012 International Research Journals *ISSN: 2076-5061* www.scholarjournals.org

Jadhav. N.S. (2010)*Relationship between home environment & emotional maturity of college going students of Belgaum District,* International Research Journal, October 2010, ISSN- 0975-3486 RNI : RAJBIL 2009/30097 VOL I * ISSUE 13

JohnLouis R and Doss Manoharan I. Christie. (2007). Emotional Maturity of Post-Graduate Students in Pondicherry Region: Experiments in Education. Vol. XXXV, No.8.

Kaur, M. (2001). A study of emotional maturity of adolescents in relation to intelligence, academic achievement and environmental catalysts. Ph.D Thesis, Punjab University, Chandigarh.

Kaur, M. M. (2013, january). A Comparative study of Emotional Maturity of Senior Secondary School Students. International Indexed Referred Reseach Journal, 48-49

Kour, J., & Arora, B. (2014) Coping styles among teachers trainees in relation to emotional maturity. IMPACT: International Journal of Research in Humanities, Arts and Literature, 2(4), 29-34.

Kumar, S. (2014) Emotional Maturity of Adolescent Students in Relation to Their Family. International Research Journal of Social Sciences, 6-8.

Kumar, T. V. (2012) A comparative study of emotional maturity among 8th to 12th class Students with the reference of internet surfing. International Indexed & Refferred Research Journal, 4(37), 8-9.

Leung J. & Sand M. (2000) " *Self-Esteem and Emotional Maturity in College Students*", Journal of College Student Personnel, Mayer, 8(1), 27–37.

Mahmoudi.A. (2012) Emotional maturity and adjustment level of college students. *Education Research Journal* Vol. 2(1): 18 -19, Available online at http://www.resjournals.com/ERJ

Passer, M. M., & Smith, R. E. (2009). Psychology: The Science of Mind and Behavior (4TH ed.). New York: McGraw-Hill Companies, Inc.

Nuzhat. J. (2013) "Emotional Maturity of Male and Female Kashmir University of India Distance Learners-A Comparative Study", Journal of Culture, Society and Development- An Open Access International Journal ,Vol.2 2013

Punithavathi. S. (2013) "*Emotional Maturity And Decision Making Styles Among Arts And Science And Engineering College Women Students*",Asia Pacific Journal of Marketing & Management Review, ISSN 2319-2836 Vol.2 (4), April (2013) Online available at indianresearchjournals.com

Roma Pal, K.M. (1984)"*Manual for Emotional maturity Scale*", Agra Psychology Res Cell. Agra.

Sharma.B. (2012) Adjustment and Emotional Maturity Among First Year College Students. *Pakistan Journal of Social and Clinical Psychology*, Vol. 10, No 2, 32-37

Sinha.V. (2014) A Study of Emotional Maturity and Adjustment of College Student. *Indian Journal of Applied Research,* Volume: 4, Issue : 5 ,ISSN - 2249-555X

Sivakumar. R. (2010) "A study on attitude towards democracy in relation to social and Emotional maturity", Ph.D, Thesis, Annamalai University.

Stephen. S. (2002) "*A study related to neuroticism and emotional maturity among college female*", Unpublished,Ph.D. thesis, Osmania University, Karnataka, India.

Strongman K.T. (2003). The psychology of emotion (5TH ed.). New York: John Wiley & Sons Ltd.

Subbarayan.K, Visvanathan.G. *(2011)*A Study on Emotional Maturity of College Students. *Recent Research in Science and Technology, 3(1): 153-155 Volume1 ~ Issue 4 pp: 15-18, ISSN (Online):2321-9467*

Walter, D. and Smithson W.S. (2002). The Meaning of the Psychology of adjustment current concepts and application, New York: McGraw Hill Book Co. Watson, & Williams. (2002, July).

Printed by Libri Plureos GmbH in Hamburg,
Germany